POLITE PROTEST

Richard B. Pierce

POLITE PROTEST

The Political Economy of Race in Indianapolis,
1920–1970

INDIANA UNIVERSITY PRESS
BLOOMINGTON AND INDIANAPOLIS

This book is a publication of

Indiana University Press
601 North Morton Street
Bloomington, IN 47404-3797 USA

http://iupress.indiana.edu

Telephone orders   800-842-6796
Fax orders   812-855-7931
Orders by e-mail   iuporder@indiana.edu

© 2005 by Richard B. Pierce

The paper used in this publication meets the minimum requirements
of American National Standard for Information Sciences—Permanence
of Paper for Printed Library Materials, ANSI Z39.48-1984.

Manufactured in the United States of America

Library of Congress Cataloging-in-Publication Data

Pierce, Richard B.
    Polite protest : the political economy of race in Indianapolis, 1920–
1970 / Richard B. Pierce.
        p. cm.
    Includes index.
    ISBN 0-253-34587-1 (cloth : alk. paper)
    1. African Americans—Civil rights—Indiana—Indianapolis—
History—20th century.   2. African Americans—Indiana—
Indianapolis—Politics and government—20th century.
3. Indianapolis (Ind.)—Race relations.   4. Indianapolis (Ind.)—
Politics and government—20th century.   I. Title.
    F534.I39N43 2005
    323.1196'073077252—dc22   2004014816

1 2 3 4 5 10 09 08 07 06 05

TO LEIGH, FOR EVERYTHING

CONTENTS

ACKNOWLEDGMENTS

I enjoy music, particularly jazz, perhaps because of that genre's ability to embrace improvisation and dissonance. In many ways, those that helped me along the way reflect the same characteristics. So many individuals and groups offered encouragement and assistance along the way that it is impossible to note them all, but I appreciated each encouraging word or gesture without which this manuscript would be diminished in some immeasurable way. And like a jazz composition, each note was indispensable.

While at Indiana University, I was fortunate to study with Richard J. M. Blackett and James H. Madison. As advisor, mentor, now colleague and friend, each steadfastly held me to task while providing encouragement and example. Their influence and friendship continue unabated. Also at Bloomington were a group of friends who have continued their roles as readers and critics, among them Paul Murphy, Debbie Gershenowitz, Matt and Sarah Vosmeier, Meg Meneghel, Lynn Hudson, Jane Rhodes, Jeffrey Ogbonna Ogbar, Priscilla Dowden, Earline Rae Ferguson, Ron Gifford, and Chana Kai Lee. I am grateful that their comments were often combined with good coffee.

As I traveled to conduct the research necessary for this manuscript, many friends provided me comfortable lodging. Among those, I thank Mary and Anastasio Gianoplus in Virginia and Scott Beasley and Liann Tsoukas, who shared their home with me while I was in residence as a Fellow at Carnegie Mellon University. Late-night conversations along with playing with their children provided clarity and balance. Governor Joe Kernan and his wife, Maggie, shared their condominium with me while I researched in Indianapolis. Many members of my extended family provided restful accommodations and great food. For their generosity, I remain grateful.

Wilma Gibbs was my tour guide through the voluminous collections at the Indiana Historical Society and other repositories that held information relevant to my study. Wilma's interest in my project went well beyond that of an archivist; she would often share her insightful interpretations with me and I came to trust her judgment and discernment. Robert Sloan and his colleagues at Indiana University Press have been conscientious colleagues. I appreciate their forbearance. Timothy Kenny's maps grace the fourth chapter, creating a stark image to represent residential change. He has been a helpful colleague. My research assistants, Arienne Thompson and Shawtina Ferguson, diligently did that necessary work to ensure accuracy and consistency. Along the way, they also provided needed humor. Lisa Harteker was an excellent editor. I will always be grateful to her for the excellent counsel she provided. I cannot imagine having written this book without her.

At Notre Dame, a number of colleagues generously set aside their work to help me with mine. Ted Beatty, George Marsden, John McGreevy, Walter Nugent, Emily Osborn, Cheryl Reed, Thomas Slaughter, and David Waldstreicher read significant portions of the manuscript and made valued comments. Myrtle Doaks's influence cannot be overstated. I appreciate their camaraderie.

Thankfully, there is an extended network of African American scholars that provide mentoring and camaraderie. I have relied on their generosity and guidance. I am happy to be among their number and hope to be as helpful to them as they have been to me. There are some like Joe Trotter, Stephanie Shaw, Fanon Wilkins, Felix Armfield, Cheryl Hicks, Nichole Rustin, Tiwanna Simpson, Patrick Mason, Hugh Page, Alvin Tillery, Toni Irving, and Don Pope-Davis who along the way made me laugh and think. For a project such as this, it was necessary to have people that inspired laughter and thought.

Tera Hunter epitomizes the ideal scholar colleague. She helped me understand this project in ways that I had never considered. Her generous and warm spirit transcends any category I could invent. I am grateful for her friendship.

Many members of my family did not understand my devotion to this project. Nonetheless, they believed in me and provided emotional and material support. My mother, Erlin, and father, Richard, instilled a vision of a world without limits. I strive to do the same for my children and hope that in doing so I can repay them for their sacrifice.

No one sacrificed more for this book than did Leigh Anne Hayden. We have known each other since childhood and the evolution of our relationship is the great joy of my life. She is my friend, defender, partner, and motivator. This book is for her because she was the first believer.

POLITE PROTEST

Introduction

John Tucker was murdered on July 4, 1845. In life and death, Tucker was not a man of lasting historical significance. He was not a statesman, an athlete, or a crusader. He was a man that had purchased his freedom from slavery and lived an unobtrusive life in Indianapolis, Indiana, where he was murdered on a downtown street by a gang of men who were celebrating their independence. Two hundred people witnessed Tucker's death and some heard voices saying, "Kill the d—d nigger, kill him!" and "The niggers are gitting too thick, and they ought to be thinned out."[1] Police officials made one arrest.

During an intense portion of the 1951 Indiana high school basketball tournament, Crispus Attucks High School principal Russell Lane nervously watched his Tigers compete with Anderson High School for the regional title game. While people in the stands worried over who would win the contest, Lane feared a confrontation between the white players and fans from Anderson and the African Americans that made up his team and fans. The Indiana High School Athletic Association had only recently allowed "colored" schools to play in its annual tournament, and the last thing that Lane wanted was an emotional contest that sparked an outburst that could risk their place in the tournament.[2] He wanted the team's access to translate into greater social opportunities for the city's African American population.

Lacking sufficient funds, Kamau Jywanza withdrew from Clark Atlanta University in Atlanta, Georgia, in 1968 and returned home to Indianapolis. Jywanza had been active in the Civil Rights movement while at Clark and assumed he would continue his involvement at Indianapolis's new state university campus. But the city he had grown up in seemed unchanged. "There was nothing. Nothing. Indianapolis was dead. It was as if the Civil Rights movement wasn't going on."[3]

If Jywanza sought demonstrations in the street or acts of civil disobedience, then he was not fully aware of the city's history. The few blacks that were in Indianapolis when John Tucker was murdered did not take to the streets or publicly denounce his murder. Given their small number it would have been unreasonable and unsafe for African Americans to respond too demonstrably. Instead, a group of white abolitionists led by Reverend Henry Beecher raised funds to hire two lawyers to prosecute the one unlucky man picked from the mob as Tucker's murderer. Public protests centered on racial issues were not part of the city's political landscape. African American protest efforts were at times so desperate that African Americans hoped the efforts of high school basketball players would ameliorate their condition. Discussions affecting the city often took place behind closed doors, negotiated settlements hammered out by black and white city leaders, far from the public's view. Indianapolis citizens had long established a tradition of face-to-face dialogue and lengthy committee deliberations to confront the city's racial challenges. That tradition led to agonizingly slow reform. So slow, in fact, that many residents believed no reform was underway. Throughout the twentieth century, Indianapolis's African Americans engaged in a never-ending struggle for increased civil rights. The result was a negotiated freedom, one that was a product of a seemingly constant contest between African Americans and their allies and the forces that preferred a city replete with discrimination and limited civil rights for black citizens.

In 1821, the Indiana General Assembly approved the site at the confluence of White River and Fall Creek as the state capital and adopted the name Indianapolis for the city. At the time, there was no newspaper or postmaster and no locally elected officials. The White River was not even navigable, making Indianapolis the only state capital not located on a navigable river. A mere 224 city residents voted in the county election in 1822. There was so little development at the site that Corydon, a town on the Ohio River, continued to serve as the state capital until 1825. Capitalistic development did not create the city; rather, the city's geographic appeal was the lone deciding factor. The confluence of the river and creek was the geographic center of the state and supposedly reachable by the state's inhabitants regardless of where they resided, a circumstance that prevented Corydon's continued role as state capital. In 1827, the city in the middle of the state had 1,066 residents, 55 of whom were African American. From the city's inception, then, African Americans were present. The contours of the city and the African American population developed simultaneously.

One of the more intriguing challenges facing early city leaders was the formation of an antebellum city that housed a significant number of African Americans. The embryonic African American population had demonstrated their desire to remain in Indianapolis with the construction of Bethel African Methodist Episcopal Church in 1836 to serve their religious needs. Despite the state's bald attempts to rid itself of African Americans through the efforts of the Indiana Colonization Society, and more dramatically with Article XIII of the state constitution, which promised to bar additional African Americans from moving to Indiana, blacks continued to move into the state and its capital city. At the onset of the Civil War, 498 African Americans constituted nearly 3 percent of the city's population. The large Union military presence drew slaves from Kentucky and Tennessee who were unwilling to wait for formal emancipation. By 1900, 15,931 blacks lived in the city (9.4 percent). Indianapolis, then, had become a city with a significant African American presence. Such was not the case for many large northern cities that commonly absorbed African Americans. In those cities, African Americans could more justly be termed migrants. In Indianapolis, however, African Americans were as much natives of the city as any other inhabitant of a nineteenth-century midwestern town, and the distinction is crucial, for because of their early presence they possessed a historical memory of the city's promise and direction. By the early decades of the twentieth century, and certainly by 1927 when schools were officially segregated and a host of other Jim Crow rules existed, African Americans believed that the city had departed from its promised course, and the recognition of the departure ignited and fueled subsequent protest. Moreover, some whites joined African American protest efforts because they too possessed a historical memory of the city's promise.

The African American community developed differently in Indianapolis than it did in places further north. Instead of receiving the bulk of its African American population during the World War eras, Indianapolis already contained a sizable African American population as the city itself developed, and it maintained a significant population throughout the twentieth century. Accordingly, African Americans were not an addendum to the city-building process; rather, they were an integral component of the city's political economy. Due to their long presence in the city, and particularly because of the integrated secondary schooling present until the late 1920s, African Americans were able to form relationships with whites, some of whom later occupied seats of power. Whites and blacks were not strangers to each other in the early days of Indianapolis, but they did occupy different strata within the city. After World War I, with the nation awash in nativist sentiment and the re-emergence of hate groups like the Ku Klux Klan, racial segregation and discrimination in Indianapolis increased. But despite rising separatism, blacks still felt they could regain lost rights through adherence to public decorum and civil protest. Fully cognizant of their history in the city, they devised their method of protest: protracted negotiations, interracial coalitions, petition, and legal challenge. Such polite protests, they believed, would allow them greater civic and personal freedoms while not antagonizing whites and thereby ensuring additional deprivations.

Scholars have been reluctant to characterize African American political dialogue as negotiations because blacks seemed to have so little power to bring to the negotiating table. Further, the term implies that two equal parties met to determine an agreed-upon direction or course of action. Clearly that was not the case in Indianapolis's early history, as whites had economic and political advantage in almost every circumstance. Yet despite the numerous examples of inequality, blacks were participants in the creation and maintenance of Indianapolis. Moreover, as Indianapolis leaders became increasingly concerned with the city's national image during the twentieth century, blacks and their disadvantaged status in the city threatened the positive, modern civic image leaders attempted to cultivate. African American experiences might portray Indianapolis as a southern-style city complete with segregation and Jim Crow statutes, a daunting prospect for civic and commercial leaders who hoped to increase the city's economic fortune by claiming otherwise.

It is more difficult to explain African American participation in negotiations with members of the city's power structure. African Americans worked within the system primarily because they were reluctant to jeopardize their gains through active, disruptive civil disturbances. They were cognizant both of the inequalities they lived with daily and the gains they had made. Whites tolerated their presence and were not routinely or overtly hostile. It would be condescending and incorrect to argue that African Americans settled for the status quo, for they continued to press for reform and advancement. Rather, it is more accurate to say that African Americans made a decision to make their place better while retaining their gains. Consequently, African Americans regularly eschewed radical, abrasive forms of protest.

Most historians of the northern African American urban experience have studied the migration of blacks from the rural south to urban centers and the communities they created there. In contrast, this study examines the experiences of African Americans in Indianapolis after they had been in the city for two generations or more, a period that historian Thomas C. Holt characterized as one of "adjustment, adaptation, and struggle."[4] Such conditions probably characterize all of African American history. Beyond enlarging the time frame of urban African American history, this study is important because through an examination of Indianapolis we learn how a city in the lower Midwest, one with a large African American population, created a style of race relations and protest that, if not uniquely the city's own, is emblematic of the style preferred in that region.[5] To date, much of our understanding of urban black populations emanates from cities in the north that underwent significant population adjustment as blacks hurried to the region during the Great Migrations of the early and mid-twentieth century. Equally confining, knowledge has come from studies of southern cities where both racial dynamics and legislative history differed greatly from those of cities in the Midwest.

My analysis begins in the early twentieth century and extends through the

Civil Rights and Black Power era. Instead of defining the black community by a mere accounting of its inhabitants, I define Indianapolis's black community by what it did—by how it worked to construct the political and social culture of the city. That this community encountered hardship along the way is not surprising since that was the situation for blacks in nearly every urban environment. The methods they undertook to eradicate the barriers presented them are the substance of this book and, in many respects, the essence of the community. For too long the urban experience of those in the largest urban centers has stood as the de facto description of the African American experience. *Polite Protest* will contribute to a more comprehensive picture. Indianapolis's geographic location (less than 100 miles from former slave states), combined with a significant number of black residents when the city was in its infancy, created a different history than that of cities such as Milwaukee, Chicago, and Detroit, cities that matured without a significant black population. We have been unwise to let stand the perception that the political economy of cities in the lower Midwest developed along the same arc as their better-known northern cousins. It is not enough to say that Indianapolis was different—for every city has its own particular history. What is necessary is to reveal the dynamic negotiations of this city's people, both black and white, as they created their own platforms and patterns of racial relations in the public and cultural spheres.[6]

In many ways, Indianapolis's African Americans appeared to be a model community. In addition to their eschewal of violent protest, the community demonstrated educational advancement, encouraged home ownership, and practiced hard work and thrift. When compared to other African American communities in neighboring states, African Americans in Indianapolis routinely outpaced them in quality of life measures.

Blessed with model African American citizens, Indianapolis chose to marginalize and demean African Americans through policy measures that restrained African American liberty. White civic leaders actually increased segregation measures through the 1940s. In 1969, those measures culminated with the effective reduction of African American voting power with the creation of Unified Government (Unigov).

White resistance took the form of policy and legislation and, like African American efforts, was not overtly confrontational. After the waning of the Ku Klux Klan's influence in the mid-1920s, civic leaders found it much more productive to preserve the status quo through Jim Crow policies rather than tolerating extreme groups that threatened stability. Despite repeated African American initiatives to alleviate policies that were harmful, a succession of white leaders chose to work with the White Supremacy League and other groups dedicated to the segregation of races.[7] Perhaps they did so because they did not fear radicalism from the African American community. The African American community that could state in 1931 that it was as "righteously proud of the U.N.I.A. [Marcus Garvey's nationalist organization] as the N.A.A.C.P." was unlikely to foment rebellion.[8] White civic leaders set an agenda to marginalize African Americans in the public domain while maintaining harmonious, peaceful race relations. This book documents the determined effort whites exerted to maintain a segregated city as well as African Americans' unwavering response.

The best example of white determination to pursue racial exclusion is seen in public schooling. Indianapolis had an integrated school system, at least at the secondary level, until 1927, when the school board created an all-black high school, Crispus Attucks. The school board's decision to create a race-based high school where none had existed before reflected the white community's increased concern with a large African American community that had grown even larger after World War I. Both Attucks's construction and the subsequent protest put African American spokesmen in the unusual position of negotiating with former schoolmates, now city officials and business leaders, about the virtues of integrated education. They offered their own civility and patriotism as examples of the types of citizens produced in the city's heretofore integrated high schools. On a personal level, African American parents who had graduated from integrated schools had to tell their children that only one public high school welcomed them. One can only assume that the children questioned their parents about the changed policy. What had they done to be stigmatized so severely? I cannot imagine the parents' answer. The creation and longevity of Crispus Attucks High School demonstrated the inability of African Americans to parlay their numerical strength into a powerful deterrent to the limitation of civil rights. The fight to desegregate schools united poor and wealthy blacks in an extended struggle to win access to quality schooling and perhaps more importantly to prove to their children that they were not some contagion others must avoid. Above all, and despite the dedicated protest efforts of African Americans, the effective segregation of schoolchildren until the early 1960s, despite the 1949 state law prohibiting race-based student placement, highlighted the white community's overwhelming support of racial exclusion.

The African American population in Indianapolis was of such size that it occupied three separate, non-contiguous residential neighborhoods in the city. Each neighborhood reflected the time of settlement in the city, but neighborhoods came to represent class differences as old-time settlers were conscious of their increased "civility" and material holdings. The size of Indianapolis's African American population made the incremental, amoeba-like growth of most northern urban African American communities untenable.[9] The greater part of chapter 3 explains the lengthy struggle African Americans undertook to secure sufficient, quality housing in the Indianapolis metropolitan area and vividly displays the patient, often painstaking negotiating process they encountered. Indianapolis's ever-growing African American population continually challenged the city's residential and racial restrictions. Their determined effort to engage in a non-destructive dialogue with city leaders was partly due to their desire to preserve the neighborhoods they inhabited. One resident succinctly, albeit resignedly, summarized the depth of feeling regarding his housing when he lamented, "Well, we like it here better than Georgia. We at least live better."[10] Despite the frequently dilapidated condition of many homes in African American neighborhoods, many also believed that they had it better than African Americans located in nearby cities. During the early decades of the twentieth century, Indianapolis residents, black and white, lived with fewer occupants per dwelling on average than did residents of Chicago, Louisville, Cincinnati, or Columbus, Ohio.[11] Protracted discussions were frustrating, but negotiations did not physically threaten their homes in the manner that public protests might have.

The study also examines African American efforts to break the wall of white labor solidarity. They hoped for more than what a 1930s era woman wearily prophesied for her children when she lamented, "Well, they'll just be laborers, that's about all. . . . I've just about given up. It has been so hard."[12] The varied protest efforts in the labor market were always about jobs and expanding economic opportunity. Progress in the labor arena was difficult because negotiations between blacks and whites had typically occurred in political arenas. Labor jobs, in particular union jobs, were initially outside the realm of political influence. Nevertheless, African Americans were able to make some headway because of their tight association with the Democratic Party and its sway with union leaders. Historian Kenneth Kusmer has argued that African American urban workers faced deteriorating occupational fortunes, especially in manufacturing jobs, in the early decades of the twentieth century and that this predicament led to lower home ownership numbers.[13] Indianapolis's African American population, while facing discrimination in the labor market, was more widely dispersed in the marketplace than African American populations in nearby communities. African American protest efforts resulted in uneven chips in the wall of white labor solidarity.

Perhaps nothing more symbolizes the bittersweet process of negotiation more than the city's political orientation. Indianapolis changed its city governance twice within a 100-year period; the first reorganization disposed of the ward representation system in favor of an at-large model and the second reorganization created Unigov, which brought the city and county under shared governance. I argue that whites supported each governmental reform because in addition to the organizational and economic benefits, reorganization promised to mitigate the political strength of the large African American population. In each case, one could reasonably assess that African American loss was a byproduct of reorganization. While much of the book talks of the negotiation that took place between white and black citizens, especially at the political level, the enactment of Unigov demonstrated the weakness of the African American community's political position, its overdependence on the Democratic Party, and its inability to parlay significant voting strength into a vital component of the city's political constituency. Repeated changes in the very political structure of Indianapolis inhibited the African American community's economic fortune by limiting the community's political strength.[14]

African American history is, at its core, and especially during the twentieth century, a study of black protest. Most of the scholarship of protest focuses on confrontational battles pitched on city streets, in parks, and along waterfronts.[15] Boycotts and sit-ins attract the public eye and the historian's research. It is human nature to seek the dramatic and the explosive, the seismic events that mark change. However, African American protest was not so monolithic. Large, long-standing African American populations were a constant factor in the political calculus of urban communities. As was the case in Indianapolis, where there were small immigrant populations, African Americans occupied an enhanced position in political negotiations. Consequently, I contend, such cities developed a negotiation process among their white and black citizens and appointed representatives that made confrontation unlikely and unproductive. Blacks were able to maintain the posture of a civil, patriotic, and hard-working population deserving of full civil rights while not risking their many accomplishments by engaging in loud public disturbances. Such an approach allowed white city leaders to grow a city without fear of massive civil unrest. The Chamber of Commerce promoted the calm race relations in Indianapolis in national magazines in an effort to attract businesses and economic development. They marketed Indianapolis as a "100% American city," where people owned homes, went to work during the week, and prayed on Sunday. African American and white city leaders, for often differing reasons, were willing to participate in protracted negotiations because it was the course of action that allowed them to preserve their city.

1

More than a Game

The Political Meaning of High School
Basketball in Indianapolis

African Americans in Indianapolis endured inequalities in housing, education, employment, and a host of other quality of life areas familiar to students
of African American urban history. Faced with enduring inequities, African
Americans struggled with fundamental questions that had plagued African
American communities for a century or more: How best to protest their circumstances and advance their community's sociopolitical and economic condition? Which strategies would bring relief and advancement without also
bringing reproach and backlash? African Americans realized there were structural impediments in Indianapolis, legal and extralegal, that constricted their
opportunities, none more important than the at-large voting system that determined city council members. African Americans from Newark to Oakland,
Detroit to New Orleans recognized similar restrictions, but the methods employed to combat these structural impediments were unique to each locale.
Whether or not to protest was not a realistic question. Accounts of creative
African American protest methods are legendary in history, literature, and folklore. The only question was which methods and what areas to combat.

Histories of African American communities in the United States analyze migration streams, community formation, and exploits of agency. Historians have
usually focused on the varied processes through which African Americans took
root in cities and the forces that aided or hindered their development. Recently,
however, historians have studied non-traditional forms of resistance as effective means of individual and community development.[1] Robin Kelley popu-
larized the phrase "infrapolitics," resistance that occurred outside of formal
channels, usually in full view of the oppressor yet without his awareness that
subversive activities were afoot.[2] By its very nature, infrapolitics is a desperate
measure engaged in by people who are cut off from formal political avenues.

While Kelley's southern subjects were often without formal political resources, Indianapolis's African Americans had open access to the ballot and coalition building. Perhaps their struggle would have been easier had they lacked the franchise, for such a condition was a ready and convenient explanation of the inequalities that typified their lives. Nevertheless, despite their voting power, African American Hoosiers resorted to clandestine protest to advance their political and civil rights. Much of this book details the repeated efforts African Americans undertook to gain equality in specific areas only to endure rebuke by a dominant white society determined to preserve the unequal status quo. However, this chapter lays bare how desperate African Americans were to change their life circumstance, so willing to force change, that they employed infrapolitics on the grandest scale and placed their hopes on the shoulders of a group of seventeen- and eighteen-year-old young men. The analysis centers on an event, the 1951 high school basketball tournament. The event occurred near the chronological center of my study, but it serves as a gateway to understanding race relations in Indianapolis and the nature of African American protest.

Beginning around the Civil War, Indianapolis struggled in a series of fits and starts to define itself as a city. The Civil War had a profound influence on life in Indianapolis. Before the conflict, one could aptly characterize the city as a sleepy burg in the middle of nowhere. One of the few state capitals not located on a major waterway, Indianapolis had a difficult time becoming a commercial center. Most livestock and agricultural commerce in the Midwest traveled through Cincinnati or Chicago. Historian Frederick Kershner identified the Civil War as the "greatest catalytic agent of urbanization in Indianapolis history."[3] During the Civil War, Indianapolis became a site for military deployment. Railroads began to move human and material cargo to and from the city. What had been a liability, namely Indianapolis's geographic location, became an asset. The city boasted of its central location between the settled East and the developing West, its relatively flat terrain, and its easy accessibility. One observer prophesied continued growth: "[T]welve railroads come through this little town . . . and their number will increase to fifteen before the end of the year."[4] Many of the soldiers who visited Indianapolis decided to make it their home at the conclusion of the war. Both farmers and industrialists saw the economic advantages of a centrally located city with a vast railroad network that could easily transport their goods anywhere in the country. By the end of the war, city boosters proclaimed that Indianapolis was the "greatest inland city in America" and would soon become the "great manufacturing city of the country." Later they would boast that Indianapolis was at the "crossroads of America." In five years, Indianapolis had undergone a major transformation in capital and influence. No longer undesirable or unreachable, primarily due to the expansion of railroad services, the city now occupied an important position in the economic fortunes of the Midwest.[5]

The early decades of the twentieth century found African Americans in Indianapolis struggling to validate their presence while powerful forces conspired to block or curtail their entry into the main arenas of city life. They must have wondered how they could be so limited in a city in which they had such a strong numerical presence. Mirroring the pattern set by African Americans in Chicago, Detroit, and New York, Indianapolis's blacks were segregated within the spatial, economic, social, and political structures of the city. In each city, blacks challenged existing limitations. Indianapolis's blacks faced a unique challenge primarily because of their significant presence in the city. Already by 1900, blacks made up nearly 10 percent of the city's population, and by 1910, Indianapolis had the sixth largest African American population (21,816) among United States cities. Under the pretext of creating a more efficient municipal system, city voters in the early 1890s reformed the system of representation on the city council when they moved from a ward system of representation on the city council to representation drawn from at-large voting. The measure removed any realistic opportunity for blacks to seat a representative on the council.[6]

Indianapolis's business leaders, most notably Eli Lilly, head of the Indianapolis Chamber of Commerce and founder of Lilly Pharmaceutical, also had a disproportionate impact on city development.[7] As they did in other cities throughout the United States, Indianapolis's leaders adopted a business approach to municipal government that emphasized efficient operation and decentralization. The Chamber of Commerce took the lead in providing advice to elected officials, and they were forthcoming in their assertion that businessmen provided the best leadership for city development. Leaders in the black community recognized Indianapolis's penchant for relying on non-elected officials and adopted a reform strategy that worked at the highest levels with little direct involvement of working-class and poor people. Their strategy, too, was a direct reflection of the at-large voting system. There was little benefit in currying favor with community members that could not elect ward representatives. Hopeful African American political leaders were better off currying favor with Republican and Democratic city leaders, the individuals who could place them on the ballot. African Americans needed to look no further than the at-large voting system to understand their Jim Crow status in Indianapolis. Despite their large presence, they did not have commensurate political influence, a circumstance that would not change until well into the twentieth century.

Indianapolis had three distinct black areas. The largest and best-known was an area directly north and northwest of downtown Indianapolis, called Pat Ward's Bottoms. The Bottoms, so named because it was close to the often dank and smelly canal, was also near Indiana Avenue, which became the cultural center of the black community. During the day, the street was the center for commercial activity, with retail stores lining both sides of the street, and in the evening, it was the location for social activities. The "Avenoo," as it was termed by residents, was the African Americans' Main Street. Along the street, patrons entered businesses confident of receiving fair, courteous service. Indiana Avenue was so replete with services that its presence helped insulate the black community from the harsher aspects of racial limitations in the city. By the early decades of the twentieth century, African Americans owned many of the businesses on Indiana Avenue, the most notable of which, because of the national sale of its hair care products, was the Madam C. J. Walker cosmetic factory. Born Sarah J. Breedlove, Walker moved her company's headquarters from St. Louis to take advantage of Indianapolis's central location and good access to railroads. Walker reportedly was the first black female millionaire in the country, and the Walker Building, completed in 1927, nearly six years after Walker's death, anchored Indiana Avenue and housed a movie theater, the Walker beauty shop, drug store, coffee shop, and numerous offices.[8]

Like other northern industrial cities, Indianapolis faced labor shortages during World War I. African American migration to the city increased to meet this need, and white Indianapolis residents became concerned about the growing presence of African Americans in the city. During the 1920s, blacks constituted the largest and, for many whites, the most threatening ethnic minority group in Indianapolis. Between 1870 and 1920, the black population doubled in number. In the period between 1910 and 1920, the black population grew from 21,816 to 34,678, a 59 percent increase. In 1920, blacks constituted nearly 11 percent of the total population.[9]

It was during the 1920s that discussions of creating a high school solely for African American students intensified, and the result, Crispus Attucks High School, opened its doors in 1927. Crispus Attucks was perhaps the most visible form of segregation in the city, but it was not the only evidence of Jim Crow in Indianapolis. African Americans held some jobs nearly exclusively, they attended separate churches, had separate cultural and social organizations, and could not participate fully in the city's amusements such as parks or restaurants. They could not stay in hotels and had to take care not to get sick in too great a number, for only a single ward at Indianapolis City Hospital was reserved for them. The lure of decent jobs that had brought so many African Americans to the city proved illusory: Indianapolis employers and union officials were among the worst violators of equal rights in the United States.[10] While Indiana did not have as complete a system of Jim Crow as many African Americans remembered in their southern homes, it did have its own unique brand of discrimination.[11]

Within this social and political context, and cognizant of the city's cultural contours, African Americans pressed for civil and political reform. The varying methods are analyzed in the following chapters, but surely the most creative approach was through the use of sports. The widespread presumption that success in sports reflected well on a group's character and potential for citizenship shaped the understanding of Attucks's success in 1951 and inspired a range of responses.[12] African American leaders in Indianapolis self-consciously worked to parlay athletic achievements into more tangible gains. Their successes and failures reveal the measured pace of racial progress in Indianapolis.

Why basketball means so much to Indiana residents remains unclear, but the game has become central to the identity of many of the state's residents. James Naismith, who invented the uniquely American game of basketball while teaching in Massachusetts, claimed shortly before his death in 1939 that "[b]asketball really had its origin in Indiana, which remains today the center of the sport."[13] African American communities throughout the United States had long debated the use of sports to advance civic and social causes. Most notably, the *Crisis* and *Opportunity,* the respective media organs of the National Association for the Advancement of Colored People (NAACP) and the National Urban League, advocated intercollegiate participation in sports as a way of displaying time-honored qualities of sportsmanship, loyalty, "manly character," and courage. The editors at the *Crisis* and *Opportunity* thought such participation would place historically black educational institutions among the "first rank" of colleges and universities.[14]

In the case of Indianapolis and the Attucks Tigers, however, African American leaders sought to elevate the entire African American community to the first rank of citizenship. The participants of the basketball tournament were playing a game, but to others, especially the elders in the African American community, the tournament was a political activity, a visible protest against the African American condition. Given that Hoosiers felt they owned the game, African Americans increased their civic identity by playing interscholastic basketball. Their participation in the game, coupled with their eventual success, intertwined them with the larger Indiana community in a manner that transcended mere residency. Crispus Attucks High School represented the African American community in Indianapolis. Churches and social clubs unquestionably served specific segments of the community, but Attucks appealed to the whole African American community. The *Indianapolis Recorder,* the African American weekly newspaper, helped the African American community claim the school by enthusiastically publicizing Attucks events. Through the *Recorder*'s effort, the African American community was kept well abreast of the social, athletic, and academic events that took place at Attucks.[15]

Such institutions were needed in a city in which the municipal code called for enforced racial segregation. Despite its deleterious effects, segregation gave African Americans some responsibility for creating their own entertainment, their own space. It was a circumscribed opportunity to be sure, but one that blacks eagerly grasped. African Americans in Indianapolis were no different from their counterparts around the country, and they, too, defied the utterances of some pastors and visited local streets where jazz clubs and dance halls dominated. African Americans in Indianapolis traveled to Indiana Avenue, home of numerous clubs and saloons, to while away the evening and straighten up after a week stooped at labor. Howard Owens fondly remembered Indiana Avenue during the 1930s and 1940s. "You could walk through the Avenue and get anything you wanted. Friendship . . . entertainment . . . anything. There were people everywhere, all along the sidewalks and even in the street. You could go there at three on a Saturday afternoon, stay there until two Sunday morning, and have a real blast. Even if there had been TV in those days, we wouldn't have watched it . . . we had too much running to do."[16] It was also along the Avenue, on the hard-packed dirt basketball court at Lockefield Gardens housing project, that the best pickup basketball games in Indianapolis regularly took place.[17] Drawing black youngsters from around the city and a few adventurous whites, the court at Lockefield Gardens, called the Dust Bowl long after asphalt covered the dirt, was a proving ground for future Attucks basketball players.[18] Thus, activities that occurred in segregated spaces were essential components of the community's culture.[19]

Members of the community, especially its young ones, developed self-esteem on the sporting field.[20] Crispus Attucks, as the only high school for blacks in Indianapolis, brought all the members of the African American community together. The recent migrants and the old-timers, those with limited means and those with greater wealth, all sent their children to Attucks. The teams the school fielded represented the economic diversity present in the African American community at large. In a way not always found in churches or social clubs, Attucks and its sports teams represented the African American community more completely than did any other public entity.

Nevertheless, Attucks was still a segregated institution, segregated even in interscholastic athletic competition. The Indiana High School Athletic Association (IHSAA), the state's ruling body of high school sports, ensured that segregation by refusing to grant Attucks membership. The IHSAA counseled member schools to refrain from playing schools that were not part of the association.[21] While full membership was supposedly open to all public high schools in Indiana, the IHSAA refused full membership to private, parochial, fraternal, and all-black schools until 1942. Member schools could receive a dispensation to compete against non-member schools for holiday tournaments, but teams rarely sought dispensation for a game during the regular season. Consequently, Attucks competed against the two other all-black schools in Indiana, Roosevelt High School in Gary and Lincoln High School in Evansville, parochial schools around the state, and similar schools as far away as Illinois, Missouri, and Oklahoma.

The IHSAA's actions contradicted its founding constitution, which stated simply that membership was open to public high schools of the state. Any public high school in Indiana offering and maintaining three or four years of high school work was to be considered a member of the IHSAA if it followed the rules and regulations of the organization and paid annual dues. A special section detailed the fate of "colored schools." Colored schools desiring to join the IHSAA were to be granted limited memberships that allowed them to play member schools under certain circumstances, not including IHSAA-sanctioned tournaments.[22]

Excluded schools, particularly parochial institutions, continued to pressure the IHSAA to change its rules. The organization's objection to blacks playing in the state tournament seemed indefensible. Integrated schools throughout the state included blacks on their athletic rosters. Ray Crowe, future head coach at Crispus Attucks, was the only black player on Johnson County's Whiteland High School team, where he played during the early 1930s.[23] Increasingly, African American players participated on integrated teams throughout the state. Evidently, the IHSAA did not exclude black schools in an effort to prohibit African American participation, but rather because they followed the segregationist stance adopted by some school systems in the state. Schools that had been denied full membership in the IHSAA continued to badger the organization for full admittance. Parochial schools and the few remaining all-black schools joined forces to demand a change to the IHSAA's exclusionary policies. In 1941, Howard M. Hill, president of the IHSAA Board of Control, alerted member schools that the executive board was studying the possibility of allowing all state high schools to join the organization.

Finally, in 1942, thirty-eight years after the IHSAA began operation, it opened its doors to every four-year state high school. The IHSAA simply revised its official handbook to read, "Membership in the Association shall be open beginning August 15, 1942, to all public, private, parochial, colored and institutional high schools of the state offering and maintaining three or four years of high school work provided they meet the requirements of the Association and also subscribe to its rules and regulations."[24] Crispus Attucks no longer had to travel to Louisville or Oklahoma to complete a full basketball schedule. They were free to compete against any team in Indiana that chose to play them. Yet, despite the IHSAA ruling, Indianapolis schools continued to omit Attucks from their regular-season schedules. The city schools' decision to avoid scheduling games against Attucks typified Indianapolis's increasingly stratified structure. Attucks was forced to travel to rural Indiana towns to play against teams that viewed it as a visiting novelty act, a high school version of the barnstorming Harlem Globetrotters. Their seemingly freewheeling style of play was foreign to communities whose teams favored numerous passes and set shots.[25] However, the Attucks players and their style of play were not foreign to their city neighbors. There, they were not a novelty act, but there is little evidence that the other high school teams feared Attucks or saw them as a possible powerhouse. Rather, city schools dismissed Attucks as unworthy competitors. The second-class status ascribed to African Americans made their scheduling appear normal. If sport held the promise to elevate one to respected citizenship, then it was reasonable to exclude blacks from competition. Regardless of the IHSAA's actions, the racial politics in Indianapolis did not allow schools to compete against Attucks. They had long ago relegated Attucks to the Bottoms.

By 1951, Attucks's position as an institution serving only the African American population was brought into question because of the success of the Attucks basketball team. The team had lost only one game during the regular season and was poised to do well during the state championship tournament. Advancement through the tournament, which included every high school team in the state irrespective of size, was not assured.[26] Despite being the largest city and the state capital, Indianapolis had yet to produce an excellent basketball team. A city school had advanced to the state finals only three times before 1951. Year after year, teams from the hinterlands had journeyed to Indianapolis to play the championship game, which was a painful experience for Indianapolis citizens. Despite Attucks's regular season record, Corky Lamm, sportswriter for the *Indianapolis Star,* did not pick Attucks to advance beyond the first round of the tournament. He was not alone. Many skeptics in Indianapolis believed that Attucks's relatively weak schedule and their recent arrival to the school-boy tournament portended a quick departure from the field.[27]

The Indianapolis sectional took place at Butler Fieldhouse, the same location as the state championship game. High school students from throughout the city considered the Butler sectional, as it was called, the highlight of the school year. One female student from Shortridge High School described the sectional as all-consuming: "You lived, breathed, imbibed and just camped out at the Butler Fieldhouse. It was a social experience. It was a total cross-section of Indianapolis." A student from Washington High School recalled simply, "The sectional was everything. The event of the whole year." Throughout the city, high school administrators allowed students to leave school to attend the sectional.[28]

As Attucks continued to win game after game during the sectional weekend, it became apparent that they were going to represent the city the following week at the regional level. There was an eerie silence at the Fieldhouse as the whites in the audience realized that a group of African American students would represent the city in the ongoing state tournament. There was little for Attucks's opponents to do except listen to the Attucks's followers sing their "Crazy Song":

> Howe thinks they rough;
> Howe thinks they tough:
> They can beat everybody,

but they can't beat us!
Hi-de-hi-de, hi-de-hi;
Hi-de-hi-de, hi-de-ho;
That the skip, bob, beat-um;
That's the Crazy Song!

The song, born at a time when Attucks was not allowed to play city schools and sung to the tune of Cab Calloway's *Minnie the Moocher,* took on new relevance in the waning moments of the game long won. Attucks's fans were telling the rest of Indianapolis that their supposed inferiority was now proven false. They had long known they could compete evenly with city schools if given the chance. Attucks's team, drawn from segregated neighborhoods in every part of the city, was now the sectional's representative at the next stage of the tournament.[29]

During the regional tournament, Crispus Attucks was announced as Indianapolis Crispus Attucks, since the custom was to identify first the city and then the school. The team's success in winning the sectional caused many white Indianapolis residents to do considerable soul searching. Indianapolis was one of the few districts in the state that still relegated African American students to one school despite a 1949 law that made segregated schools illegal.[30]

Therefore, an all-black team represented the city in the state's most important schoolboy tournament and threatened to do what had never been done: bring a state basketball championship to the city. Some whites were afraid that an Attucks victory would lead blacks to riot, either in celebration or in protest of their condition. After the sectional victory, Lamm, the *Star* columnist, chided his readers by asking, "Attucks won the Sectional and the city's seams didn't come apart, now did they?"[31] Lamm may have mildly scolded his readers for their fears of rioting fans, but he also consoled them by predicting that Attucks would never beat Anderson High School, a perennial power from nearby Madison County, in the next round.

While whites in Indianapolis were still a little unsure about whether to wholeheartedly adopt the Attucks team, the city's African American community was not ambivalent. The celebration after the sectional victory was a curious affair. For many, the immediate goal had been won. Attucks had shown Indianapolis that it could compete favorably against every team in the city. In a basketball-crazed state, and in a city starved for a dominant team, a sectional victory was occasion for celebration. African Americans swarmed to Indiana Avenue. Traffic nearly came to a standstill as cheering fans danced in the street. Perhaps some fans feared that this celebration might be the last, as Anderson was indeed a formidable opponent. The location of the celebration further signified that the team belonged to the African American community. When the team finally paraded down the street, a throng hardly foreign to them embraced them. These young ambassadors had done for the community what no amount of previous agitation had done. They held the city's focus. No longer relegated to the city's "bottoms," Attucks had moved the African American community to center stage.

Despite the prospect of a local state champion, Attucks fever failed to infect the larger Indianapolis community. Of the sixteen regional sites, Indianapolis and Lafayette were the only two that did not sell all their tickets, an unusual occurrence even when no Indianapolis teams were among the regional contenders. Only a week earlier, the total attendance for all the tournament sectionals had topped a million for the first time in history. With one exception, *every* city radio station broadcast a tournament game.[32] Many of the regional site coordinators had to hold a lottery to equitably allocate tickets to all those who desired entry.[33] The efforts undertaken by the regional site coordinators testified to the tournament's statewide popularity, but the unsold tickets at the Indianapolis regional indicated that Attucks's appeal was limited. Ticket sales lagged in Indianapolis despite widespread media coverage in the *Recorder, News, Times,* and *Star.* But, in contrast, no publicity was needed to stoke the enthusiasm of the African American fans. Their anticipation was so great that the team had to be sequestered at the Senate Avenue YMCA (the YMCA branch in the city reserved for African Americans), leaving only to attend school during the week leading up to the regional. Coach Ray Crowe wanted his team to get some respite from community well-wishers.

Finally, game day arrived. Two basketball coaches from the northern part of the state sped eighty miles in eighty minutes to make the tip-off, knowing that they would see a "ball game."[34] And they were right. The game was a see-saw affair. Attucks jumped out to a quick lead, but Anderson fought back and trailed by only eight points at half time. In the second half, Anderson benefited from some "suspicious" calls by the officials, slowed Attucks's attack, and took a seemingly commanding ten-point lead with four minutes to play. People had segregated after entering the Butler Fieldhouse. During the final four minutes most fans were standing. Some had fainted and photographs later showed people crying. Although Indianapolis was the site of the game, most of the cheering followed racial lines. On the court, it seemed as if Attucks was playing uphill. Attucks assistant coach Al Spurlock later said that the officiating caused him great concern: "I was kind'a scared because of the bad officiating." Years later, he added, "By the end of the game it seemed as if Anderson had seven players on the court—two with striped uniforms."[35] With twenty-three seconds to go, Anderson led 80–79. Eschewing a time-out, Charlie West, an Attucks forward, went down court with the ball. In Indiana, as in most places, scoring the winning basket is the thing of legend. West wanted to be immortal. Unfortunately, his shot went awry, and Attucks was fortunate to get the ball back after an Anderson player tipped it out of bounds.

With seven seconds left, the Fieldhouse was in a near panic as Attucks inbounded the ball. Bailey "Flap" Robertson, a substitute forward on the squad, received the ball and took a shot.[36] Later reports said the game was "without a doubt, one of the most thrilling high school basketball games ever played in Indiana—or the world." Another reporter termed the game "the most dramatic and exciting" in tournament history. There was some controversy as to whether Flap's shot arched beautifully before dipping through the rim or if it had a flat trajectory that lost momentum and simply tumbled into the net. Both scenarios provided the same outcome. Flap Robertson became immortal.[37]

After winning the regional championship against Anderson, a school touted as the one to put Attucks in its place, the team paraded down Indiana Avenue again. Somehow, the Attucks fans outdid the previous week's celebration. Traffic was at a standstill. A bonfire blazed outside of Crispus Attucks High School. People danced until dawn. Responding to the opinion of some city leaders that Attucks's success might lead the African American community to push for civic and social changes in a city where Jim Crow laws and customs flourished, the police chief sent extra patrolmen to Indiana Avenue in case trouble erupted. However, additional officers were not needed to monitor the revelers, who were far too polite in passion and protest to violate civic decorum.

The state championship games were two weeks away, but Attucks had survived its toughest challenge. The two northern coaches who had exceeded the speed limit and had the good fortune to reach the Fieldhouse believed they had already witnessed the state championship game and one of the greatest games they had ever seen. They offered encouraging praise to Attucks fans: "Attucks is a great team. It played the hardest it will ever have to play—and won it. It won't have a game that rough the rest of the way."[38] The coaches' prediction seemed eerily correct a week later when Attucks easily beat Covington and Batesville to win the semi-state. Their margin over Covington, forty points, was the most lopsided semi-state victory since 1916. Attucks was now one of four teams remaining in the state tournament. It appeared that Indianapolis might finally have a champion.

Attucks seemed to be the subject of every conversation in the days between the semi-state and finals weekend. One editorial opined, "in the Statehouse, the Courthouse, the marts of business and the homes of rich and poor, the name of Attucks is on every tongue."[39] Finally, the *Star* columnists came around and joined the Attucks bandwagon. Not only did the sports columnists predict that Attucks would win the championship, they also claimed the team as the city's representative. They saw in Attucks an opportunity for the city to have its own champion—a champion that had not played against city schools during the regular season. A champion they had wrongly predicted would lose in the first round. When Attucks won the sectional, they predicted a loss during the regional. After Attucks beat Anderson, the columnists finally accepted Attucks as their team. All prior events and dire predictions were forgotten. A column appearing before the semi-state weekend summed up the writer's glee: "[F]or Indianapolis, after 40 years of frustration, to face the rest of Indiana on Saturday and say [quoting Attucks's "Crazy Song"], 'You can beat everybody, but you can't beat us.'"[40] Miraculously, Attucks had become Indianapolis's team.

But Attucks was not an orphan up for adoption. The black community, from whom the players emanated, still held them as their own, and they had not groomed these kids to represent Indianapolis. They had fought to get Attucks into the IHSAA so that their children could compete openly against whites in a manner many adults were unable to in their everyday lives. Middle-class black commentators used the team as an example of all that was good in the black community and a visible example of the costs of segregation. The Attucks team was excelling on the most visible stage in Indiana. The team represented the African American community first, and the rest of the city second, and the players knew it. Will Gardner recalled, "We were taught from day one that if we did anything stupid, then the whole school and [Negro] community would suffer."[41] For teenage boys to carry the hopes of the community on their shoulders must have been an awesome responsibility. City newspapers commented frequently on the importance of race. The two largest dailies and the *Recorder* agreed that Attucks's standing as a "black school" should not sway city residents' emotions one way or another. Stating the obvious, yet underestimating the attachment African Americans had to the school, the papers affirmed that Attucks was part of Indianapolis. But, obviously, Attucks was a segregated space, one created through racial discrimination. Perhaps the message for the *Star* editorials was that Attucks was already a part of Indianapolis and that adjustments to the city's social and regulatory code were not necessary. The appeal for city residents to ignore that Attucks was the only city school with African American students was ridiculously optimistic. The city's African American leadership would not allow the city's residents to ignore race.

The *Recorder* considered Attucks's success as nothing less than a referendum on race relations in the city. Noting that Attucks's brilliant basketball play had aroused a "veritable tidal wave of interracial democracy," the editor believed he saw the hand of God. He wrote, "Where the appeals of religion, reason and education seem to have fallen on deaf ears, the spectacle of brilliant basketball has turned the trick. In deep humility we observe that God does move in mysterious ways."[42] It was indeed startling to see Indianapolis whites cheering Attucks, but the *Recorder* also questioned how widespread had been God's work. It asked whether Hallie Bryant, the team's versatile forward, would be able to get a job as easily as he garnered rebounds and whether Will "Dill" Gardner would be able to move as freely around Indianapolis as he did on the basketball court.[43]

The editors were not trying to mock the team's newest fans. Rather, they sought to extend the significance of the team's success to every facet of African

American life. This team, whose members came from middle-class families as well as from families who could not afford tickets to see the tournament games, stood poised as an agent of significant change. An advertisement placed by a group of interracial city leaders evinced the broad range of concerns the Tigers addressed:

> For the sake of the school, the improvement of race relations and friendly attitudes among all groups and the boosting of community morale, we heartily cheer for Attucks. And bless this team with our best wishes for a victory that will give us our first state high school basketball championship.[44]

No longer playing at the Dust Bowl for bragging rights over which side of town produced the best basketball players, the team was now supposed to improve race relations and boost the community's morale.

But despite the blessing of city leaders, Coach Ray Crowe understood that winning the championship might harm race relations in Indianapolis.[45] Crowe and some administrators at Attucks feared that Indianapolis was not ready to embrace the Attucks Tigers as its team. Whites needed more time to adjust to this all-black team from the city's west side. Perhaps if Attucks's ascendancy had not been so rapid, Indianapolis might have become accustomed to the new basketball power in its midst. But there had been no previous indication that the Tigers were going to steamroll through the 1951 regular season. It was, after all, Crowe's first season as head coach. No other city high school team would have been saddled with the charge to improve race relations. No other team required an official administrative blessing. It is further doubtful that another team would have required city residents to become accustomed to their title run. Attucks's run to the championship was as direct an assault on racial inequality as had been staged in the city. Indianapolis citizens, black and white, were unaccustomed to direct challenges to the city's racial order. Crowe and Russell Lane, Attucks's principal, thought white residents in the city needed more time to get used to Attucks's success. Reflecting the opinion of the more conservative and dominant faction of African American leaders, the men believed that the team's success threatened positive race relations. By the conclusion of the sectionals, city residents knew they had a new basketball power in their midst; by the time semi-state arrived, that very same team was labeled an ambassador for race relations.[46]

Anointing new ambassadors to fight for civic freedoms in Indianapolis was an unusual happenstance. The political culture of the black community had been identified and well-entrenched for many years.[47] Few commentators could argue that black leaders, whether Democrat or Republican, secular or ministerial, were radical protesters. The civic leaders' rejection of Thurgood Marshall's offer to make Indianapolis the site for a legal case testing the constitutionality of segregated schools typified their political style and was consistent with the manner of change in Indianapolis.[48] Rarely did African Americans forcefully demand change; rather, blacks and whites met frequently within interracial organizations, including political parties, to negotiate change in the Hoosier capital. Negotiating change in such a manner brought agonizingly slow, incremental progress—and sometimes no progress at all.[49] Frequent and sometimes frank discussions at interracial forums led many whites in Indianapolis to believe that race relations in the city were good. In adopting such a belief, whites were guilty of what historian William Chafe labeled the "progressive mystique." They confused dialogue with action.[50] Blacks, too, were accustomed to the process of political negotiation. Civility marked their interaction with the city's leadership, and for too long African Americans believed that repeated appeals to friendly whites would bring desired change.

In offering the Attucks Tigers as an example of the community's readiness for full participation in civic affairs, blacks were on the cusp of forming a new political strategy. Breaking with their tradition of relying on interracial coalition building, they now offered to go it alone by showing their deservedness. However, they were not cutting all ties to established practices. Attucks shelved their wide-open and "flashy" game during the tournament and instead played a more traditional, and slow, basketball style. In so doing, they made themselves recognizable to Indianapolis basketball fans and, by extension, proved that the dismantling of racial restrictions would not dangerously change the city's landscape. Their play and self-reliance spoke to a new front where blacks ascribed political meaning to their public activities and achievements. Moreover, blacks adhered to the long-standing precept in African American political protest that rights and freedom would accrue to those who acted respectfully and courteously. In other words, rights would extend to those that showed they deserved them.[51]

Russell Lane and Coach Crowe emphasized sportsmanship during the week leading up to the finals. Stressing sportsmanship was not necessary to this team. The players had presented no disciplinary problems and had conducted themselves admirably during the tournament when referees seemed to favor the opposing team. They had gone into hostile environments and never violently engaged opposing teams or their fans. Lane was afraid, however, that the team's victory would make players and students too aggressive in their fight for reform. He echoed the concern of others that parity on the basketball court might lead to demands for parity in other parts of society.[52]

The question, a constant in developing strategy for African American protest, was what approach would bring advancement. Perhaps author James Baldwin best characterized the dilemma facing African American protesters, and, ironically, he found the dilemma represented in sport. On assignment for the men's magazine *Nugget,* Baldwin covered the heavyweight boxing championship fight between Floyd Patterson, then champion, and the challenger,

Sonny Liston, whom most people, President John Kennedy and the NAACP leadership among them, considered a dangerous brute. Baldwin admired both men and was torn over whom to support. Baldwin wrote, "I felt terribly ambivalent, as many Negroes do these days since we are all trying to decide, in one way or another, which attitude, in our terrible American dilemma, is the more effective: the disciplined sweetness of Floyd, or the outspoken intransigence of Liston. . . . Liston is a man aching for respect and responsibility. Sometimes we grow into our responsibilities and sometimes, of course, we fail them."[53] Lane represented those who favored the disciplined sweetness of negotiation and compromise. He feared that forceful, incessant demands would destroy years of interracial coalition building and goodwill. Others, most notably Starling James, president of the Federation of Associated Clubs (FAC), wanted the team to represent a new direction in African American protest in Indianapolis.[54] James wanted a new style characterized by the same qualities the team possessed: unified, competitive, winning. Either the team could be a spearhead for change or merely another example leaders could point to when displaying the African American community's civility.

While their elders contemplated the importance and significance of the team's activities, the boys still had games to play. Lane ventured to the team's locker room before the semi-final game against Evansville Reitz. The fans were in a near-frenzy as they awaited the team's arrival on the court, and the players struggled to hear their principal over the noise coming from the stands above.[55] Lane reminded the boys of their uneasy position as ambassadors. "You are representing much more than your school," Lane said. "You are black Indianapolis. This time the whole state is watching. More important than winning is that you demonstrate good sportsmanship. Be gentlemen."[56] A curious pep talk to be sure, but it reminded the players that they were playing more than a game.

It is difficult to know for sure how many players adhered to Lane's admonition. One player, Bob Jewell, won the Trester Award that goes every year to the tournament player who best exhibits "scholar-athlete-citizen" qualities. The player he was guarding in the semi-final, Jerry Whitesell, led Reitz with nineteen points. Perhaps Jewell, who came from a middle-class family, had heard Lane too well. With most of black Indianapolis at the Butler Fieldhouse for the game, or listening to the proceedings on radio or watching on television, Crispus Attucks lost to Evansville Reitz, 66–59, in the afternoon session of the state final. Crowe realized after the game that talk of sportsmanship, and perhaps the actions of the referees, had reined in his Tigers. Years later he recalled, "We were not ready, and that was my fault. I made up my mind right then that we would be back, and the next time we would be ready."[57] However, no one accused Attucks of acting rudely. In the end they did not bring disrespect to their community, but they did not provide them with a trophy either.

But many in Indianapolis seemed not to mind that the boys came back without the championship trophy. Henry T. Ice, president of the Indianapolis Chamber of Commerce, stood at a post-tournament rally to declare, "Indianapolis proudly claims you as its own." Phillip L. Bayt, a Democratic Party leader and mayor, followed Ice and added, "You're still champions as far as we in Indianapolis are concerned. You displayed honor and sportsmanship. We would have much better citizens if all were as clean as you Attucks players."[58] The *Recorder* said it all with a headline: "Attucks Tigers Lose; But City's Civic Spirit Rises."[59]

Starling James spoke bluntly to the team when he said, "Sportsmanship cost you the game."[60] James, a relative newcomer to the city having lived in Indianapolis only fourteen years, had long been frustrated by the black community's unwillingness to fight forcefully for change. Watching Attucks lose at the hands of suspicious referees was one thing, but to add to the complicity by being too mannerly was more than he could take. Their conciliatory posture reminded him too much of the pose adopted by the larger African American community. The team's conciliation was a lost opportunity to directly confront unequal civic freedoms among Indianapolis residents. The contrasting comments offered by white and black commentators also hinted at the uneasiness with which many whites in Indianapolis came to support Attucks. Whites and blacks supported the Attucks run, but it appeared that whites were more wary in their acceptance, as if supporting the team was part of a civic responsibility and not a passion. That Ice had to tell the team, at that late stage, that Indianapolis "claims you as its own" made clear that the team had stood outside the city's consciousness before the tournament.

Herman Shibler, superintendent of Indianapolis public schools and a vocal critic of the school board's foot-dragging on desegregation, favorably assessed the significance of Attucks's run for the championship: "That basketball team accomplished more for race relations in one season than you could accomplish in ten years of forums and discussions. The white people here have a completely new impression of the colored race. It's marvelous."[61]

Angelo Angelopolous, a white reporter for the *Indianapolis News,* placed Attucks's achievement in perspective. He argued that eventually the 1951 team would be best known for its contribution to society and its conscience:

> In its march through the state high school basketball tournament the impact made by Attucks' tremendously talented team took on the aspects of a social revolution in this city of heavy Negro population. The force of Attucks ability alone in the beginning carried along a considerable number of fans here, but the spiritual impetus Attucks provided with its conduct compounded its converts until when 2:30 P.M. came last Saturday there were thousands of sad hearts in Indianapolis belonging to people who wouldn't have felt so a month before. . . . the thing the

1950–51 Attucks team may eventually be known for—its long step toward making Indianapolis one town.[62]

The remaining question is whether these players, and their efforts, really did help to transform Indianapolis. Were Indianapolis residents able, as Angelopolous dreamed, to demolish the walls that divided their community? While efforts to desegregate Indianapolis schools continued, both a state law and the isolated position Indianapolis occupied among other cities in Indiana fueled those efforts. As more and more high schools traveled to the state finals with racially integrated teams, it was harder for Indianapolis to defend its increasingly lonely segregationist position.

Did competitive expediency fuel the increased integration at the secondary level? How did city employers answer the *Recorder*'s public question of whether blacks could acquire jobs appropriate to their skill as readily as Hallie Bryant rebounded missed shots? Would African Americans be able to move freely throughout the city, lodging and recreating where they chose without adhering to a racial code? All these questions will be answered in subsequent chapters, but African American community leaders surely believed that the 1951 Attucks basketball team had displayed the community's deservedness for increased freedoms and participation. Throughout the bulk of the book, the protest efforts employed to bring relief in education, labor, and housing are analyzed. Each arena found a similar pattern of protest, but in 1951, during the schoolboy basketball tournament, African Americans hoped to bring reform by displaying the Crispus Attucks basketball team as an example of what the community had to offer: civility, fair play, courteous deportment, and positive example. By 1950, many African Americans were veterans of protest battles; they had won some and lost many. They had engaged the disciplined sweetness of Floyd Patterson. They had not taken to the streets to voice their hatred of the city's Jim Crow practices. Instead, they worked to build interracial coalitions, they constructed reasoned and logical arguments against the separation of the races, and they protested their unequal condition in subtle and not so subtle ways. Such was the nature of African American protest efforts in this city that they hoped that the play of teenagers would bring community relief. Their strategy evinced equal parts of creativity, politeness, and desperation. Infrapolitics might bring measured feelings of individual empowerment, but African Americans fought for community redress and advancement. Indianapolis's African American community now ached for respect and responsibility. The Attucks players proved they had grown into their responsibilities and, perhaps, they had the ability all along.

2

"We Have Given You No Extremists"

The Challenge against Segregated Schools

In 1927, Indianapolis created, or more accurately recreated, segregated schools in direct response to the increased number of African American students in the city's school population. Indiana school officials held the authority to segregate schools if, in their estimation, the presence of African American children warranted the creation of separate facilities. Indianapolis officials did not have to create separate schools and by the 1920s, after nearly fifty years of integrated secondary schooling, it appeared they would not exercise the privilege the law allowed. However, beginning already in 1909, school officials began to wonder whether the large number of African Americans in the schools presented the breeding ground for civil unrest.[1] Throughout the middle decades of the twentieth century, African Americans fought segregated schools first in the meeting room of the school board, then in state and federal courts, and, finally, in the halls of the state legislature.

With each successive venue they gained and lost allies and their strategy shifted, but their goal remained the same: the removal of segregated education in the state's capital city. One element characterizes the noteworthy attempts by the city's African Americans to alter the status quo. In each instance, African American leaders pursued conservative protest strategies hallmarked by politeness, civility, and order. Their foci of protest changed as city officials repeatedly rebuked their efforts, but they continued to pursue polite protest and negotiations. In the meantime, while nearly thirty-five years of negotiations and pleading took place, scores of African American schoolchildren suffered under a policy that routinely placed them in substandard buildings with inadequate resources. The protests preserved the peace, a goal of African American leaders, but they did little to effect meaningful, timely change. African American leaders failed to appreciate that pro-segregationist forces used the slow pace of negotiations and court challenges to forestall change. The protest methods

African Americans implemented and the results they achieved form the core of this chapter.

Segregated schools existed in Indiana long before the Civil War. In 1843, the state legislature declared that blacks should be educated, but made no provisions for schooling. The legislature did, however, bar blacks and mulattos from attending public schools with whites. Left to their own devices, and wanting to gain an education, African Americans in Indianapolis often copied the educational efforts of frontier pioneers. They established private schools or hired itinerant teachers to teach community children. Their efforts did not go unnoticed by Thomas B. Elliott, president of the Indianapolis school board. At the end of the Civil War, Elliott reported that the "large proportion of colored children attending pay schools is very creditable to this people, and indicates an earnest desire for improvement."[2] A. C. Shortridge, superintendent of the Indianapolis schools, urged public schools for colored children and was impressed with African American self-help efforts. According to Shortridge:

> Their schools are maintained under great disadvantages—without the generous sympathy of the public generally, with very moderate funds, with building unsuited to school purpose, with limited or no school apparatus, with uncomfortable school furniture, with insufficient textbooks, without classification, and with teachers unskilled in the art of imparting instruction. In our judgement humanity, justice, and sound public policy demand that this class of our citizens shall receive the benefits of our common school system.[3]

African Americans had proven that education was of such importance that they were willing to pay for the privilege.

In 1869, the Indiana General Assembly enacted a statute that allowed blacks to attend public schools, but the statute also allowed local officials to create separate schools for blacks if they so desired. Indianapolis school officials acted in concert with the state and allowed African American students to enter the public school system while availing themselves of the option to designate student placement by race. For the next fifty years, Indianapolis children attended segregated elementary schools, but, for those who passed an entrance examination, an integrated high school experience ensued.[4]

In 1895, Gabriel Jones, a black state representative from Indianapolis and himself a teacher, introduced a bill that permitted children to attend the school nearest their home. Under the bill, a trustee who discriminated based on race or color was guilty of a misdemeanor. The Indiana House of Representatives passed the bill, but the Senate pocketed the proposal, thereby allowing trustees to continue discrimination based on race.[5]

Jones's bill divided more than the Indiana legislature: Indianapolis's black community also split over the bill. Some black teachers regarded the Jones bill as a threat to their livelihood even though the bill did not prohibit black schools, at the time the only schools where black teachers were employed. Thirty African American teachers signed a petition against the bill, arguing it would deprive them of their livelihood. A counterpetition led by Robert Bagby, a former schoolteacher, insisted that the black community strongly supported the measure because "Indiana alone of all the northern states keeps up this discrimination against colored children." The employment of black teachers would remain a central issue in the long struggle for desegregation. Teachers occupied a unique position in the black community as symbols of its potential, and they were important members of the educated middle class. In this instance they were conflicted because efforts to eradicate race-based education, theoretically an improvement on the current system and a benefit for the race, could lead to their unemployment. Educated African Americans during the Jim Crow era most likely worked in the teaching, social work, and ministerial professions. While one could argue, as Bagby did, that restrictions imposed on schoolchildren translated into employment and professional restrictions for adults, too few teachers were ready to risk their personal security for the race's advancement.

African American newspapers also entered the debate over the Jones bill. George Knox, publisher and editor of the *Indianapolis Freeman,* opposed the Jones bill, agreeing with teachers that their jobs were in peril. Editors of the *Indianapolis World* disagreed, implying that Knox's stance had more to do with his attempt to curry favor with Republican officials and his aspirations for political appointment than with his concern for teachers.[6]

The impasse left Indiana with a complicated and sometimes contradictory educational policy. School systems could build separate schools for black children, but were not required to do so if the black population was not large enough to warrant additional construction or if the community did not want to segregate schoolchildren. Conversely, a community with a small number of African American school-aged children could build a separate school if it desired. While Indianapolis had race-based elementary schools, it had chosen not to construct a race-based high school.

Although always a small number, some black children did share schools with whites in the early years of the twentieth century. The number increased during World War I, when the opportunity for economic advancement spurred African American migration to Indianapolis. Largely because of an increased African American presence, white citizens began to call for more rigid barriers, particularly codified ones, to separate the races.

Segregation did not play a prominent role in the 1922 school board election campaign. Under state law, Indianapolis citizens chose the school board in a non-partisan election. Two slates competed in the 1922 election. The Better Schools League, made up mostly of incumbent members, contended that the sitting board had implemented progressive policies in the face of "unfair and bitter" opposition. Members of the Better Schools League cited improved buildings and equipment and increased teacher salaries as examples of the incumbent board's effective management. The Citizens League, citing the same evidence, charged that the current school board was wasteful and extravagant. They promised better stewardship and a curtailment of unnecessary building programs. Better Schools League candidates urged a tax levy for the construction of additional schools, while the Citizens League candidates offered no definite proposal other than a moratorium on tax bonds, the money from which was used in new construction. A tax levy for new school buildings became the central issue in the 1922 election.[7]

Curiously absent from both platforms was any significant discussion of school segregation. Both groups held similar views regarding racial separation, and perhaps neither group thought segregation a major or contentious issue. But to the victor would go the challenge of dealing with an increased population of school-aged children and petitions advocating increased segregation as the best means of dealing with the "Negro problem."[8]

The electorate voted to cast their lot with the Citizens League. Almost immediately, the new board began discussions aimed at instituting a policy of racial separation in Indianapolis schools. The speed with which they acted on the issue suggests that although little campaign rhetoric was devoted to school segregation, the issue was uppermost in the board's plans. Almost as quickly, opponents organized to fight the board's proposals. The Better Indianapolis Civic League proffered a petition, read by Robert Lee Brokenburr, a black lawyer active in the NAACP and later a Republican state senator, defending integrated public education. The petition read in part, "We emphasize that no one section of the population can be isolated and segregated while taking from it the advantages of the common culture." The Better Indianapolis Civic League was not a lone voice. At the next meeting of the school board, another delegation of blacks representing the local NAACP, a ministerial organization, and several civic groups made an impassioned plea against segregated education.[9] The speed with which African Americans formed the Better Indianapolis Civic League and coordinated the responses of various organizations indicates that they were not entirely surprised by the board's actions. Theirs was the first attempt at protesting segregated schools, and they chose a method readily available and familiar to them.[10]

Despite African American objections, the school board decided to implement its plans to segregate schools more aggressively. Charles Barry, president of the school board, claimed that the board's efforts addressed the issue of overcrowding in schools. Further, he claimed that other black citizens had led him to believe that a separate school would not be "distasteful." The *Indianapolis Freeman* indicated that black children were "being driven out of white schools" and calculated that soon there would not be a black child in a white school in the city.[11]

The *Freeman* was a little premature in its prediction. Although the 1924 school board did institute a policy of segregation, it was the school board elected in 1926 that fulfilled the *Freeman*'s dire forecast. In the 1926 election, the Ku Klux Klan actively supported the Republican Party and the United Protestant Clubs of Indianapolis ticket. In 1925, Klan members had circulated flyers calling for "White American supremacy and the segregation of Negroes, especially in the schools." Nevertheless, United Protestant Club candidates claimed they owed their allegiance to no particular group and promised to support policies that were forward-looking and progressive. As in earlier elections, candidates from both parties failed to raise issues concerning race and segregation.

But Klan influence was readily apparent in the 1926 local elections. The Klan was rumored to be associated with the state's Republican Party, but Republican officials, understandably, denied any connection between the two groups. The Klan, equally aware of the negative effects their association could have on Republican efforts, denied any affiliation with the Republican Party. Nevertheless, George S. Elliott, Exalted Cyclops of Marion County Klan No. 3, presided at a political rally that did little to squelch rumors that his organization had a vested interest in a Republican victory. Before a crowd estimated at 7,000 people, Elliott clearly identified the Klan's preference: "We are here in the interest of the United Protestant Clubs of Indianapolis." Notwithstanding prior claims that the Klan did not speak for the Republican Party, the rally ended with an introduction of each Republican and United Protestant candidate.[12]

Klan influence may have reached its zenith in the 1926 election just as Klan strength was being undermined following the murder indictment of Dwight C. Stephenson. Stephenson, Grand Dragon of the Indiana Realm and one of the highest-ranking national Klan leaders, had promised that if convicted he would name political officials who were both corrupt and linked to the Klan. He kept his promise. The Klan's fall from grace did not end segregated education in Indianapolis, but the school board brought to power largely through Klan support could not distance itself from the organization and suffered a terrible defeat in 1928 against Citizens Council candidates.[13]

In the area of segregation, board members elected in 1928 differed little from previous boards. They dictated that all "colored high school pupils" should attend Crispus Attucks, the new high school for African Americans. They also authorized the construction of three new colored elementary schools. By 1929, thirteen of the ninety-one schools in the Indianapolis school system were designated for black students. Most often, blacks were transferred to older buildings in neighborhoods whose racial composition had changed. Predictably, the school board relocated white children to newly constructed school buildings. Some black parents requested new schools for black elementary schoolchildren because present schools were dilapidated, but one should not misinterpret parental actions. Black parents who on the surface appeared resigned to segregated schools simply wanted their children educated in adequate buildings. Their request for new construction was not a sanction of segregated education, but an effort to secure the best possible learning environment for their children under the circumstances. African American parents frequently protested when their children were transferred from white to colored schools when the transfer meant longer traveling distances.[14]

In the end, the Klan was merely one of the architects of Indianapolis's segregated schools. The policy of segregation was instituted before Klan-supported candidates took office, continued while they were in position, and was maintained after they were ostensibly removed from the school board. The simple but unpopular explanation is that the majority of white voters wanted segregated schools. Faced with a seemingly ever-increasing black population, whites created formal, structural barriers.[15]

From its inception, the new high school for African Americans was controversial. The school board initially intended to christen the school Jefferson High School, but Crispus Attucks was adopted after members of the black community objected to the school's being named after a former slave owner and offered the Revolutionary War hero as a more appropriate namesake. A few weeks after Attucks's opening in September 1927, the *Indianapolis Recorder* printed an editorial acknowledging that, while some blacks had asked for a Negro high school, the vast majority of blacks were opposed to the idea. Facilities at white high schools were vastly superior to those at Attucks. Moreover, claims that the new school would provide employment for blacks was a "small and selfish contribution that means little or nothing to the vast Negro population of this community." The *Recorder* bemoaned the school's creation but wished the school well and hoped that while in existence it would at least try to provide a valuable service to the community. Using a theory akin to hating the sin but loving the sinner, African Americans reluctantly tolerated segregated schools and worked simultaneously toward the seemingly paradoxical goals of bringing about the system's demise and establishing an award-winning Negro high school.[16] African Americans never threatened to boycott Attucks or forcibly challenged the extension of segregated schools. Instead, they wanted Attucks to be an example of African American community achievement through excellence in education and extracurricular activities.

After a decade of fighting the creation of the school through three successive school board elections, blacks finally accepted Attucks as a part of the community while never resigning themselves to the school's permanent station. Given the tenor of the times and the policies of the board, it is not surprising that Attucks had to endure many of the same hardships experienced by the community. All the white schools enjoyed better facilities than Attucks's. The new building that had been constructed to house Attucks was used for a white school instead, and Attucks was moved into a vacated facility. Inequity did not end there. Black teachers were paid less than white colleagues, even when they had higher levels of education or more teaching experience.

Despite the initial lukewarm reception from the black press, Attucks quickly became a vital institution in the African American community. By 1934, seven years after opening its doors, the sixty-two-member faculty held nineteen master's degrees and two Ph.D.s. The percentage of advanced degrees held by Attucks's faculty far exceeded that of any other high school in the city. Nor did excellence end with the teachers. Students soon filled clubs, a newspaper staff, and athletic teams. Joseph Taylor, who attended an all-black school in Missouri, remembered competing against Crispus Attucks in football and basketball in the 1930s: "Those teams were good. Nothing was worse than traveling all the way to Indiana to play Attucks and then having to ride the bus back to Missouri. They didn't just beat you. They beat you up."[17] Willard Ransom played several sports for Attucks in the 1940s and recalled the feeling of community that existed on the athletic teams. Seven classmates on the football team later enrolled at and competed for Talladega College in Alabama after graduating from Attucks. An alumni association actively promoted the school to the community and published a newsletter detailing the exploits of its graduates. Although few African Americans initially supported Attucks's creation, many community members who had no direct association with the high school helped it become a visible symbol of excellence within the community.[18] Student loyalty to Attucks was rarely in question. One student recalled his feelings when riding the bus directly past Shortridge High School to reach Attucks: "I never felt bad about going to Attucks. I felt sorry for those people having to go to Shortridge." Glenn Howard, Attucks class of 1958, recalled, "It was just a friendly atmosphere to have people come from all over the city to attend Crispus Attucks High School."[19] Born out of segregation and discrimination, Attucks established itself firmly as a viable African American institution.

Attucks had a black principal and a black teaching staff. No other school in the city was similarly situated. Colored elementary schools uniformly had white principals. The *Indianapolis Recorder* recognized the inequity and urged its readers to elect an African American member to the Indianapolis Board of School Commissioners. An African American presence on the school board, they believed, would insure some representation of the community on the board. The African American penchant for seeking reform through electoral politics should not surprise anyone familiar with early-twentieth-century urban communities. With their sizable population, electing a representative sensitive to their needs was a practical goal and one in keeping with their overall philosophy to amend rather than aggravate. Their electoral efforts, which they repeated frequently during the ensuing years, met with failure. The Citizens Council was too powerful and community support for an assault on its policies was lacking. Support from the black community was lacking largely because of the split within the community. For years, the *Recorder* lamented the split between the "leaders and the community."[20] Longtime residents of Indianapolis must have wondered if time was going in reverse. Those who had attended school in Indianapolis in the early decades of the twentieth century had done so in an integrated high school system; now they watched their children enter school buildings whose pupils were determined by race.

Ironically, it was a disaster that provided the first post–World War II opportunity to challenge the race-based nature of schools. During the Christmas holiday recess in January 1946, flames consumed a black elementary school, PS 63. By the time firefighters brought the fire under control, the building was no longer in any condition to house students, and 325 displaced pupils needed immediate relocation. Many local black and white leaders thought the timing propitious for changing race-based school designation. Lowell Trice, president of the NAACP branch, Faburn DeFrantz, Executive Secretary of the Senate Avenue YMCA, Freeman Ransom, General Manager of the Madam C. J. Walker manufacturing firm, and members of the League of Women Voters, the YWCA, and the American Legion met at the Senate Avenue YMCA to discuss possible solutions to the recent catastrophe. Previous school boards had routinely rejected petition protests from African Americans and their organizations, so Trice and DeFrantz determined that the group had to contain both white and black members if its proposals were to carry any weight with the school board. DeFrantz and Trice thought that the inclusion of whites would give their appeal greater standing before the school board. Interracial coalitions became a mainstay of future African American protests, but they, too, were largely unsuccessful. Organizers proposed distributing the ill-fated school's pupils among the three neighboring schools, and principals from the three white schools near PS 63 agreed to accept the displaced students. The solution was both simple and cost-effective. Having come to what they felt was a logical solution, the unnamed coalition took its proposal to the school board for adoption.[21]

But Citizen Council members still dominated the school board. For two decades, the school board had turned back all efforts aimed at desegregating the schools. Faced with its first significant challenge to desegregation in nearly twenty years, the school board reacted to PS 63's demise in predictable fashion. Working as quickly as DeFrantz and Trice's group, the board voted to transport most of the displaced children to a previously abandoned building nearly ten miles away. PS 26, a black elementary school, would absorb those who were not bused. The school board authorized a ten-room expansion project for PS 26, already the largest elementary school in the city, and summarily rejected the proposal offered by the DeFrantz-Trice coalition.[22]

Chagrined, school board opponents did not forsake the fight. Appearing before the school board, a delegation that included Walter Frisbie, state chairman of the Congress of Industrial Organizations (CIO), Rabbi Maurice Goldblatt of the Jewish Council on Community Relations, several white Protestant ministers, and the usual cadre of black leaders demanded the school board justify its decision to relocate black children ten miles away from their homes. Carl F. Brandt, president of the school board, assured the delegation that the decision to remove children from their neighborhoods had not been made in haste. The board thought it best to keep the "family of pupils" from PS 63 together. Brandt pointed to three letters received from parents of pupils as evidence that the board had acted correctly. He pulled one from the small stack and read, "As it is well known that #63 is one big happy family[,] we are happy that the faculty and children are still together." In actuality, Brandt had read only a small part of a longer letter that requested improved facilities at the "colored" school. One by one, members of the delegation urged the board to reconsider its decision, emphasizing the disruption caused to parents and children and the cost of new construction. The *Recorder* joined the fight, urging Indianapolis to profit from Gary's experience and integrate the schools before racial "agitators" brought division to the capital city. The board was unconvinced.[23]

Desegregation advocates may have lost the battle over PS 63, but in many respects they gained a victory that would stand them well in the long fight for integration. Few whites had recognized the depths to which the school board would go to maintain the present construction of race-based student placement. White moderates especially were jolted when the proposal to relocate displaced black students to three nearby schools where the principals welcomed them was rejected out of hand. The coalition that formed never took a name, but its loose alliance continued for years. The League of Women Voters, in particular, did not waver in its support. Fay Williams, among other things a member of Non-Partisans for Better Schools, recalled that "[t]he League of Women Voters were very important allies to me. Information that I needed access to, I could get from one of those nice League ladies, who appeared to be innocuous, right address, right color, graduate of one of the seven sister schools usually."[24] Although the school board would later alternately claim that residential patterns or costs dictated placement, the 1946 experience convinced many that race was the sole determinant.

Members of the school board must have begun to rue the Christmas season. Almost a year after the fire at PS 63, another petition to end school segregation was presented to the board. The petition was submitted by Jay T. Smith, a black World War II veteran and spokesperson of the Veterans Civil Rights Committee, who expected to be heard if only because of the 50,000 members he represented. If Smith believed numbers alone would prevail, he was wrong, for the board did not respond until Smith sent it a second copy of the petition. Faburn DeFrantz, Walter Frisbie, and Rev. R. T. Andrews, minister at Mount

Zion Baptist Church, all of whom frequently attended school board meetings, accompanied Smith.

Veterans were not acting out of altruistic concerns for youth. Vocational training, covered under the GI Bill, was offered at area high schools, and inferior facilities at segregated schools limited the opportunities available to black veterans. Smith's petition held that the separate but equal policy permitted by state law was not equal. The petition also confronted the persistent problem of African American teachers. "A fully integrated school system, with a fair proportion of Negro teachers and administrators should be retained, and no teacher or administrator should be dismissed as the result of this change."[25]

While school board members could previously point to fissures within the African American community—teachers hoping to retain their privileged position, students wanting to stay with their neighborhood mates, or the schism between new settlers and longtime citizens—those fissures began to close. In the post–World War II period, African Americans consistently spoke harmoniously when calling for the end to race-based student placement. The war veteran's experience with the implementation of the GI Bill may have provided the last cohesive element, for it bridged the generational gap in a meaningful way. No longer was the action of the school board pertinent only to children or families with children; its reach now extended into the economic world of adult men.

The board responded as they had nearly a year earlier, even citing their previous action concerning PS 63. They maintained a statutory right to authorize student placement with regard to race, an authority that extended to veterans. There was no intention to increase the number of racially mixed schools, as demonstrated by the board's decision to rebuild PS 63. With the board standing firm, opponents knew they now had to take the fight to another level, and so they shifted their focus to the state legislature. Because local officials had proved so intransigent, opponents hoped representatives from areas that had ended school segregation would help lead the fight for a state law prohibiting school segregation.[26]

Prospects for a sympathetic intervention by the Indiana General Assembly appeared bleak. In their 1946 campaign platform, state Democrats had included provisions for a strong public accommodation law, a more effective fair employment practice law, and an end to discrimination in public education. Their Republican opponents, who eventually swept the November election, were silent on the same issues. But there was some slight evidence that there might be some sympathetic members among the state's legislators. Robert Lee Brokenburr, the only black member in the state Senate and senior among black Republicans in the state, successfully introduced a bill that would prohibit any person or organization from disseminating "malicious hatred by reason of race, color or religion," and provided penalties for violations. In essence, it was a precursor to modern-day "hate speech laws." The bill passed unanimously in the House and the Senate.[27]

With this modest success, anti-segregation advocates, who usually expected nothing from the General Assembly, began to believe that the political climate was not as bleak as they had feared. James Hunter, a black Democrat representing East Chicago, tried to capitalize on Brokenburr's success by introducing a bill for the creation of a governmental unit entitled "State Commission Against Discrimination in Education." The commission was to examine the differences in education for white and black children and, Hunter hoped, recommend integrated schools. Unfortunately, Brokenburr's bill had proved to be the exception that established the rule. The Committee on Ways and Means buried Hunter's bill in committee. Republicans supported Brokenburr's bill more because of the prevailing rumor that the Ku Klux Klan was experiencing a revival and less because of any commitment to better race relations. Hunter's bill was a different matter. Its adoption would have taken away the latitude local school boards enjoyed in choosing to establish segregated schools, and there was no locality in the state where the issue had greater political significance than Indianapolis.[28]

African American state representatives from Marion County made one more attempt at a legislative remedy. Republicans William Fortune and Wilbur Grant, a former officer in the Indianapolis NAACP, sponsored a bill prohibiting segregation in all public schools, including state colleges and universities. Among other things, the bill stated that two years after adoption schools would discontinue enrollment on the basis of color, and pupils already enrolled in segregated schools would have the option of transferring to another school. The bill was referred to the Committee on Education, where the prospects were better than in the Ways and Means Committee. While the Committee on Education studied the problem, activists on both sides of the issue attempted to garner public support.

Again, a biracial group led the way. The Church Federation, an interfaith group representing many churches and synagogues in Indianapolis, helped write the bill sponsored by Fortune and Grant. In 1947, Henry J. Richardson, representing the Provisional Council for Unity, which included the NAACP, CIO, and a large number of church and civic groups, supported the measure. Richardson pointed out that Indianapolis was the only large northern city that maintained a segregated school system. The maintenance of such a system, he argued, was both expensive and immoral. With the influential Church Federation as a co-sponsor, members of the Provisional Council for Unity believed the Fortune-Grant bill was assured passage.[29]

Virgil Stinebaugh, superintendent of Indianapolis public schools, opposed the Provisional Council's efforts. At a public hearing, Stinebaugh read a message from the Indianapolis Board of School Commissioners reiterating their position, "without attempting to present a brief either for or against the policy of segregation in the public schools." For Stinebaugh, issues of morality did not and should not enter discussions on segregation. Rather the "question of segregation in the public schools involves many factors of community wide significance. It cannot be considered wisely without reference to current local practices in race relations in business and industrial life, in religious and fraternal organizations, recreational and character building agencies, and in neighborhood agencies."[30]

If segregation was widely practiced throughout the city, why, Stinebaugh asked, should schools be forced to desegregate? In essence, Stinebaugh implied that the whole apple was rotten. It was a brilliant move. By singling out schools for reprimand by the legislature, supporters of the Fortune-Grant bill had ignored numerous other examples of segregation in Indianapolis. Aware that the Church Federation supported the measure, the board pointed an accusatory finger at religious organizations that practiced segregation. Stinebaugh's claim was firmly rooted in his knowledge of the city. A 1951 survey sponsored by the Church Federation reported that almost half of the "white" churches responded "Not Welcome" to the query, "Are members of other races welcome at your congregation?" Moreover, by widening the spotlight to include religious and fraternal organizations and business and industrial life, the board urged citizens to examine their work and leisure lives. Schools mirrored the way capital city residents chose to live their lives. Liberal forces, they warned, would not stop with an attack on the school structure. Soon their attention would turn toward other social and political institutions. Stinebaugh further mentioned the timeworn argument that an integrated system may mean the loss of jobs for black teachers. But Stinebaugh's thinly veiled threat, one used many times over the preceding decades, was finally losing its effect on black schoolteachers. A survey of 300 black teachers found that 80 percent favored the outright abolition of segregated teaching staffs. Of course, the board's warning that African American teachers might teach white children under the new system carried considerable weight among white residents.[31]

Such was the debate outside of the capitol building. Inside, the Committee on Education debated the issue in private session. James Hunter, the African American Democratic representative from Gary, feared that the committee would bury the bill in the same way the Ways and Means Committee had killed his previous proposal. To pre-empt such a move, Hunter moved that the bill be brought to the floor without a recommendation from the committee. But the House, voting along party lines, tabled Hunter's motion. The Fortune-Grant bill suffered a similar fate, with the Committee on Education acting as their colleagues in the Ways and Means Committee had. Having tried and failed at the state level, proponents of integration had to find another avenue to directly challenge the Indianapolis school board. The *Recorder* wasted no time in establishing blame for defeat of the two bills. They proclaimed that the recently enacted anti-hate law should be used against Stinebaugh and the members of the school board. Stinebaugh's appeal to "race-hating elements in the population" was particularly galling because it appeared to have been successful.[32]

The state legislature's actions could have been predicted by a study of the demographics of the state. Cities with sizable black populations—Indianapolis, Gary, Fort Wayne and Evansville—were the areas most concerned with segregated schools. Of the four, only Indianapolis and Evansville maintained segregated systems in 1947. While these cities also housed a large proportion of the state's population, Indiana's representative districts were not proportionate to its population. Rural areas held a disproportionate number of House seats until the Supreme Court's ruling in *Baker* v. *Carr* (1962) mandated redistricting. Reapportionment finally came to Indiana in 1965, nearly forty-five years after the last adjustment. Representatives from rural areas such as Kouts or Odon, Plymouth or Brazil, derived little political benefit from voting for a school integration bill. Schools in their district were not often besieged by problems concerning race or school assignment. Many saw segregation as an Indianapolis problem that capital city residents would have to solve. That sentiment would eventually change, but in 1947 there was little enthusiasm for intervention.[33]

Blocked at the local and state level, proponents next challenged the school board through the courts and the ballot box. The latter attempt began in 1947, when three blacks were presented to the Citizens School Committee (previously the Citizens Council) as prospective candidates. One of the candidates was Roselyn Richardson, who became active in Indianapolis political struggles almost immediately after marrying Henry J. Richardson and moving to Indianapolis in 1938. Roselyn's concern stemmed from her bitter personal experiences with her oldest son, Henry III, nicknamed Bunny, who was denied entry to a neighborhood elementary school.[34] The other two candidates were Zella Ward, an active Federation of Associated Clubs (FAC) member, and R. T. Andrews, pastor at Mount Zion Baptist Church.[35]

The Citizens Committee had a membership of approximately 200, four of whom, Robert L. Brokenburr, Dr. Sumner Furniss, Willard Ransom, and Carrie Jacobs, were black. The latter two were active members of the NAACP, Ransom as the state president and Jacobs as the chairman of the education committee. Brokenburr and Furniss were longtime members of the committee and conservative in their views. Brokenburr, for instance, remained in the Republican Party long after most of his African American colleagues had departed. Included in a series of articles appearing in the *Indianapolis News*, Brokenburr was characterized as a "reasonable" person who believed things would get better eventually. He was held up as a person to be emulated. Ransom, also included in the newspaper series, was characterized as "impatient" and "forceful." Ransom was an example of the "new breed" of Negro who was both more confrontational and less desirable, at least to the editor of the *Indianapolis News*. After graduating from Talladega College in Alabama, Ransom had taken his law degree from Harvard. Both men worked as legal counsel for the Madam C. J. Walker Co. and maintained a cordial relationship. Their cordiality was demonstrated when they worked with the other black members of the committee to get Richardson, Ward, and Andrews included on the long list of potential Citizens Committee–sponsored candidates. A subcommittee of the Citizens Committee considered the large pool of applicants and then submitted their selection for ratification by the larger body. The school board election was non-partisan, but candidates usually ran as a slate.[36]

In July, as was their custom, the Citizens Committee held a luncheon to announce the candidates who would carry their endorsement. Few were prepared for the fireworks that followed. Using a table knife as a gavel, Judge John L. Niblack, vice chairman of the executive committee and superior court judge, rose to speak. He complimented all individuals who agreed to serve on the school board, a position that demanded much work and for which no member was paid. Niblack then read the names of the seven candidates, both Democrats and Republicans, chosen from a field of 150. He heard the motion for approval and waited for the customary unanimous agreement. Instead, Willard Ransom rose to his feet. Ransom asked why none of the three black candidates had been selected and what view did the candidates and the committee hold toward segregation. Proceedings came to a grinding halt.

The luncheon and subsequent announcement of candidates had become perfunctory over the years. So routine, in fact, that three-fourths of the invited guests ignored their invitation, and only one newspaper of general circulation sent a reporter. Perhaps the limited media attention explains why so many people in Indianapolis were unaware of one of the most direct African American challenges to the status quo. That the setting was a luncheon for invited guests also places African American protest in vivid relief. In many respects, the announcement of candidates had become the unofficial and de facto announcement of the school board. The Citizens Committee candidates had never failed to hold the majority on the board. Niblack paused and then judiciously stepped away from the debate, saying, "I think we finally picked out some mighty fine citizens. . . . As to their stand on segregation, you'll have to ask them. I don't know what it is."[37]

It seemed incredible to many at the luncheon that the topic of segregation had not come up in conversations with prospective candidates. Rabbi Morris Feverlicht, dean of Indianapolis rabbis and a longtime member of the Citizens Committee, emphasized that no one should be named to the school board on the basis of being a minority group member. But, Rabbi Feverlicht continued, "if you're referring to a case where a Negro child who lives in a predominantly non-Negro neighborhood must go to another section to attend school, then I'll help you fight that." Carrie D. Jacobs did not accept Niblack's answer and chose this forum to express her displeasure with the entire system. Claiming that 40,000 other blacks in the community shared her concern, she questioned the fairness of a system that forced her son to ride a bus to a segregated school instead of walking to his neighborhood school. Moreover, her son was not allowed to take advantage of special classes offered at some of the high schools. Thomas Sheerin, a member of the selection subcommittee, replaced Niblack at the podium and offered a more thoughtful answer to Ransom's and Jacobs's questions. The committee, he explained, did not want segregation to be a litmus test for candidates. To do so, he argued, would not serve the community or the Citizens Committee. A black candidate had been considered, but "the time was not yet ready. We thought we'd have a measure of difficulty carrying the candidate on the ticket." As a further example of the committee's willingness to appease blacks, Sheerin added, "We have given you no extremists, Mr. Ransom." The group then voted overwhelmingly to adopt the selection committee's proposal.[38]

Whether the committee had offered any extremists was not the issue. The seven people selected were: Dwight Peterson, president of the Cities Security Corporation; Mrs. Louis W. Bruck of Irvington, one of the prime movers in the fight to place Howe High School on the east side; H. Nathan Swain, former state supreme court judge and city controller; Leon C. Thompson, a pattern maker and partner in Thompson Bros., Inc., machine and pattern shop; Raymond F. Brandes, a south side pharmacist; Emil V. Schaad, owner of the Advance Printing Co.; and Carl F. Brandt, a contractor who was presently on the school board. Ransom and Jacobs could have charged that an extreme situation already existed, and that those nominated by the committee were simply caretakers of the existing system. Ransom recognized that no substantial changes would be made by the Citizens Committee delegation, so he moved to challenge them directly. Ransom chaired a group called the People's Committee, which nominated Rev. R. T. Andrews and Charles Preston, the only white reporter on the *Recorder,* as candidates for the board. Considering their meager budget and gargantuan task, the two candidates did fairly well; however, they were never a challenge to the well-entrenched and well-supported Citizens Committee. Again, Citizens Committee candidates swept the election.[39]

Defeated again, opponents of segregation proved that they were nothing if not persistent. Rebuked at the polls and by the state and local legislatures, the group, largely led by lawyers, took their cause to the courts. For longtime residents like Willard Ransom, a court challenge was the last recourse and the least desirable, for it placed whites and African Americans in the adversarial role that both wished to avoid. Whites avoided confrontation because they preferred the status quo and enjoyed the fact that Indianapolis had a national reputation for civility and order. African Americans avoided confrontation because for years their leaders, including Willard Ransom's father, Freeman, believed that change was possible without threatening their gains. African Americans feared antagonizing city leaders, recognizing that retribution could make Indianapolis a far worse place to live. Nevertheless, after decades of fighting a seemingly entrenched school board, the architects of patient protest realized that they could no longer avoid confrontation. But it would be fanciful to think that these exemplars of decorum could or would have taken to the streets to protest. Rather, beginning in 1947, with the country still in the flush of World War II victory and awash with seemingly unlimited power, the legal battles with the school board commenced. The legal battle would not be finally settled until well into the 1970s, after the country had fought another war.

Henry J. Richardson did not know the fight would take that long when he began. He and Roselyn attempted to enroll their two sons at a school near their North Meridian Street home, a home, incidentally, that had to be purchased by a white friend representing the Richardsons. Simultaneously, Clarence Nelson, a Methodist minister and recent émigré from Minneapolis, where he had been president of the local NAACP, attempted to enroll his daughters in PS 43, the same school targeted by the Richardsons. Both families received letters from the assistant superintendent of schools denying admittance of their children. The assistant superintendent's letter also stipulated that PS 42, a black school some distance from their neighborhood, was the proper destination for black children in that area. Neither Ransom nor Nelson was surprised by the board's decision. Their attempt was a challenge to the school board and, more importantly, an incident from which they could seek legal remedy. It was Nelson's intention all along to take the school board to court. He was in nearly constant communication with Willard Ransom, president of Indiana's NAACP branches, and Gloster B. Current, director of branches for the national NAACP.[40]

Bolstered by Ransom's and Carrie Jacobs's presence, Nelson confronted the board with his intention to file a joint suit with the NAACP charging the school board with violation of the United States Constitution. The board quickly and predictably reiterated their position that the criteria for school assignments were not race but classroom size and school conditions. The board's response was one of the early salvos in a battle that would proceed for nearly thirty years. Based on their analysis of the current situation, the board rejected Nelson's petition.[41]

Nelson's defeat spurred the Indianapolis NAACP branch into renewed activity. Their response was in keeping with their tradition of lying dormant until spurred to action by a noteworthy event. In many respects, however, the branch mirrored the reserve of the larger community. Admittance to neighborhood schools had long been denied in Indianapolis. A generation of children had never attended integrated schools, although many of their parents had.

The war years had brought more than relative prosperity to Indianapolis's black community—it had also brought a large influx of African Americans from areas other than the upper middle South; people came from locations as diverse as Washington, D.C., and St. Louis. One of the more significant migration streams came as a result of the Army finance center at Fort Benjamin Harrison. Consequently, a significant number of educated and well-placed African Americans took up residence in Indianapolis. Dr. Andrew Brown, pastor at St. John's Baptist Church and active in the local NAACP, recalled that it was finance center employees in his parish who were particularly vocal and incensed at the abuses segregation leveled on black citizens. Fay Williams, member of the NAACP and the Non-Partisans for Better Schools, who came to Indianapolis when her husband, a finance center employee, was transferred from Washington, D.C., credited the federal employees with changing the political equilibrium in the capital city. "There were a lot of blacks who came from St. Louis and Washington, D.C.: They were low grade federal employees. The fact that they were federal employees was very significant. It was job security. Coming from out of town they were much more progressive. If you had lived in St. Louis or Washington or almost any of the larger cities in the south there was a definitive black cultural experience." They made up the core (Ransom would later call them the "fighters") that forced the board to yield.[42]

But additional pressure had to be applied before the board was ready to concede to opponents. Ransom sought the aid of the national NAACP and informed them that the local branch would continue pressuring the board on the issue of segregation. Additionally, the branch made preparations to draft a desegregation bill for the upcoming legislative session. The Indianapolis NAACP branch allocated most of its resources to the school desegregation issue, a cause that dominated the branch's agenda for many years. Previously rebuked at the legislative level, Ransom now anticipated a court battle for which he wanted to provide additional evidence to any future jurist that all avenues had been explored. William T. Ray, president of the Indianapolis NAACP branch and local real estate businessman, tried to educate the new board on recent psychological studies concerning the debilitating effects of segregation and, more importantly, to remind them by his presence that the issue would not go away despite recent setbacks in the legislature. A new board member was reported to have said, "I thought that when Crispus Attucks was built we solved that problem [segregation]," to which Clarence Nelson replied, "That only started the problem."[43]

Ransom's strategy of sustained pressure began to take effect. In September 1948, the board again denied black children admittance to PS 43. This time, however, the board showed signs of wavering. While denying African Americans admittance to PS 43, the board ordered that one hundred students be transferred from an overcrowded black school to a previously all-white elementary school in a working-class neighborhood. Parents of children attending PS 32, the target school, while not opposed to their children's attending school with black children, reacted quickly to the board's new proposal by instituting an immediate boycott. Parents argued that the board was making a "laboratory" of their school and pledged to fight any such attempt unless all schools practiced integration. They also contended that they were singled out because they were less affluent than the parents who sent their children to PS 43. Until their demands were met, namely a withdrawal of the black children or full integration on a citywide basis, their boycott would continue.[44]

Henry J. Richardson stepped into the breach. He presented a plan for redistricting the school system based on the simple premise that students should attend the school nearest their neighborhood. The plan called for integration within three years. He buttressed his proposal with the usual appeals to fairness and financial savings. It would not have been a Richardson proposal unless it included an emotional appeal with a promise for additional action. "We have waited, pleaded and worked on this particular problem for more than ten years," said Richardson, "and we have personally appeared before this board six times within the last two years. We feel it high time the school throw out and abolish its old . . . policy." Failure to act promptly and correctly, he added, would result in a lawsuit.[45] Ironically, neighborhood-based education, the system espoused by Richardson, would be the mantra of the school board during the ensuing legal fight. By that time, the school board learned to make effective use of gerrymandered districts.

Indeed, Richardson and Ransom now anticipated that a legal battle would be the only remedy for such a firmly entrenched problem. Correspondence between Ransom and Thurgood Marshall, director of the NAACP Legal Defense Fund, indicates that a legal strategy had been formulated as early as February 1948. The Indianapolis lawyers hoped the city's schools would provide a test case for segregated schools nationwide. They intended to argue that segregated schools were discriminatory and that equalization of school physical plants was the only alternative to integration. Their argument was based on the premise that the school board would be unwilling to spend the millions of dollars necessary to equalize black and white schools. A risky strategy at best, it rested partly on the assumption that economic reality could sway the school board.[46]

The Indianapolis Community Relations Council hired Max Wolff, a consultant on community relations for the American Jewish Congress, to conduct a preliminary survey of the school situation in Indianapolis. Ransom believed his findings would substantiate claims of discrimination in the Indianapolis school system. Wolff's comprehensive study of the school situation found that whatever conditions may have initially justified the creation of a segregated school system, these no longer held true. He found that black children had to travel excessive distances to reach inadequate schools. Further, African American opinion had coalesced in favor of integration, and the loss of some teaching positions no longer posed a serious barrier to African American support for integration. Wolff determined that the school authorities adamantly opposed any change to the current structure because they felt public opinion dictated segregation.[47] Wolff's findings substantiated claims black parents had made for some time. The *Indianapolis Star* used the report to focus its critique of the existing system. The *Star,* a Eugene Pulliam newspaper, urged Indianapolis citizens to study the report in its entirety. If done, editors felt, any reasonable person would acknowledge that "the mixing of races in our schools is the just and economical way to run the schools." The only reason the present system existed, the editors contended, was because facts had been withheld from the populace by an intractable school board. It was only because of the school board's devious efforts that parents had felt compelled to boycott PS 32. The *Star*'s critique was a major blow to the Citizens Committee because Pulliam was widely known as an ardent conservative. Previously, Judge Niblack and his cohorts had consistently enjoyed positive support and endorsements from the Pulliam newspapers.[48] Richardson may have put it best in a letter to Thurgood Marshall: "The town is ready and ripe for the suit on the school issue."[49]

Seemingly on the brink of victory, local leaders pulled back from completion of the survey in an effort to focus their attention on a second attempt to win passage of a state law. But Thurgood Marshall felt the state legislature was unlikely to pass a school desegregation bill, and he urged local officials to push on with the survey. State and local officials politely ignored Marshall's arguments and took comfort in their knowledge of the local political scene. The 1948 election had brought Henry Schricker, a Democrat, to the governor's office, along with a Marion County Democratic delegation. Along with strong labor support, blacks had helped elect the Marion County representatives. Ransom believed the school board could not lobby successfully against the current political incumbents, taking courage from an examination of the Democrats' platform for 1948 that vowed to "work unceasingly to end all discrimination based on account of race." Marshall questioned the wisdom of this approach, but he was not in a position to countermand their course of action. He wished them well and began to look elsewhere for a situation conducive to the court challenge he desired.[50]

Marshall's good wishes were not hollow comments. Lawyers from the NAACP Legal Defense Fund were instrumental in shaping the bill that abolished segregation in public education. But Ransom's decision to eschew Marshall's legalistic approach was based on a careful examination of local political realities. Blacks, namely Henry Richardson, had helped keep Dixiecrat Strom Thurmond off the ticket in Indiana, which greatly helped Democrats win statewide office. Governor Schricker owed a debt to blacks and he went to

Richardson to pay up. Roselyn Richardson recalled the encounter between the governor and her husband:

> Governor Schricker [and Henry J. Richardson] were good friends already and had been good friends since they were in the legislature together, so the governor said, well, what do you want? And I will say for Schricker, in the light of that day, Schricker was liberal. But all he meant really when he said what do you want, he really meant, well, what committee do you want me to put your wife on, or who do you want to run the elevators in the state house. Well, Henry said, all I want is your blessing from the top for us to pass this desegregation bill statewide. He [Governor Schricker] said, what about civil rights? Henry said, no civil rights this year. School desegregation. [Schricker] What about FEPC [Fair Employment Practices Commission]? [Richardson] No, we're not dealing with the FEPC this year, we're going to deal with school desegregation. Because he knew all those tricks, you get three or four things going and then nothing happens. We already tried that and those bills got lost and nobody knows where they are. So he was determined to get Schricker's promise to do this one thing, which was to shepherd the law to prevent segregation in the schools of Indiana. That was all he wanted. And Schricker promised him. . . . And Schricker was gotten out of bed more than once when things were happening to that bill.[51]

Willard Ransom presented the bill to James E. Hunter, who by virtue of his 1948 re-election was named chairman of the Democratic caucus. Hunter still harbored resentment over the way Republicans had manhandled the 1947 desegregation bill and was eager to sponsor this latest challenge to the status quo. The Committee on Education released the bill with its recommendation, and the bill quickly passed the House by a vote of 58 to 21. Yet although it had progressed further than the 1947 bill, the newly proposed legislation still had an impressive hurdle to clear before it could become law.

Republicans dominated the Senate and had historically blocked anti-segregation legislation. Almost immediately, Republicans fell back on a tactic that had worked famously in the past. The bill was referred to the Senate Education Committee, where the previous bill had been sent and never heard of again. But Richardson and Brokenburr had also gone this route before and this time they were better equipped to fight the battle. They coordinated a public relation maelstrom. Unexpected support continued to come from Indianapolis newspapers. The *Indianapolis Times* called the existing system "needlessly expensive to the taxpayer, obviously un-American in principle, and unfair alike, to the children of all races." Cognizant of the role blacks had played in the recent election, the *Recorder* chimed in with a thinly veiled threat, promising Republicans that blacks would not forget who voted against the bill. Brokenburr, no longer a member of the Senate, exerted considerable influence in wrenching the bill out of committee. Facing unprecedented challenges on various fronts, the Republican-dominated committee released the bill with a recommendation that the Senate approve it.[52]

Willard Ransom's fears that the Republicans would not go quietly into the night soon were confirmed. Perhaps fearing that his north side Indianapolis district would become embroiled in the desegregation issue, Republican John Morris proposed two amendments that would have effectively curtailed any meaningful impact of the proposed law. His first amendment relieved school officials of the obligation to hire teachers that were of the same race as most of their pupils. Administrators, then, did not have to hire black teachers. Morris's second proposal was potentially more destructive. It provided that city councils in large cities would be empowered to determine whether kindergartens, public schools, or school departments were to be segregated on the basis of the race, color, or national origin of the pupils. Thus Morris had cleverly shifted the responsibility for desegregation from school boards to city councils. In Indianapolis, where ward representation had long since been replaced by citywide representation, the fight for desegregation would have to confront yet another formidable opponent. Assemblymen rushed to table the amendments, but their efforts failed.[53]

Nothing fully explains what followed. One historian speculated that the senators had not read the bill before voting and upon further reflection and examination chose to change their vote, a frightening but altogether common practice late in a legislative session. But it is more likely that lobbying efforts carried the day. Henry J. Richardson led a delegation to the governor's office to inform him of Morris's coup and urged Governor Schricker to exert his influence on Democratic "backsliders." Brokenburr had been equally busy among Republican senators. Ransom had NAACP delegations from all over the state come to the capitol to confront their representative. The very next day the Senate revisited the issue and voted to remove the Morris amendments from the bill. Morris tried to get an indefinite postponement, but supporters of the bill were present in full force to counter any changes or delays. House Bill 242 passed, without the crippling amendments, 31 to 5, with 13 abstentions.[54]

The *Recorder* led the cheers for the courageous act displayed by the Indiana legislature. Additionally, the *Recorder* praised the tremendous interparty, cross-organization cooperation that had produced the reversal. "A solid front of all Negro groups, with the help of liberal white organizations, was credited with bringing about the almost unprecedented reversal of action by the Senate . . . never before in Indiana's history had Negro political leaders of various parties shown such unity on a legislative measure."[55]

Individuals intimately associated with the struggle were equally gracious in their praise of each other's efforts. Andrew Ramsey, columnist for the *Recorder*, was struck by the cohesion displayed by groups heretofore at odds with one another. Ransom credited Brokenburr and Richardson with playing crucial roles as lobbyists and strategists. Ransom did not fail to recognize the efforts white organizations had made in bringing about a law that was "the greatest victory to date for the NAACP in Indiana" and a seemingly fatal wound to segregation in the state. For his efforts, Ransom received the city's 1949 Cable Award for outstanding work in race relations.[56]

Yet it took more than organizations and individuals working in concert to pass an anti-segregation bill. Local proponents confidently went against Thurgood Marshall's recommendation to proceed through the courts because they felt the political environment had changed significantly since 1947. Furthermore, some influential white citizens had begun to see the blight segregated schools caused and stood ready to relieve the city of the curse. By 1949, many Indianapolis citizens were well aware, and a little embarrassed, that the capital was the only large northern city that still maintained a segregated school system. Outsiders could point to Indianapolis as a backward city and hold the school system up as evidence of retarded thinking. Forever concerned with Indianapolis's image, Eugene Pulliam had opposed the school board's stand for that very reason. Editorials appearing in his newspapers became increasingly strident in their calls for reform. Some opponents of desegregation also argued that a segregation law was not needed because the city's residential patterns meant that neighborhood schools would be effectively segregated.[57]

Yet Ransom, Brokenburr, Richardson, et al. were also only partly correct. While the climate appeared to have changed in their favor, the law for which they had worked so diligently had a different meaning to their "allies." Cracks quickly appeared in the "solid front" when advocates of the bill tried to extend anti-segregation principles to strengthen the Fair Employment Practices Commission. Support from the Pulliam newspapers immediately evaporated and the proposed legislation died a quick death. The "coalition" was not built on ideologies of racial fairness or equality; some merely felt that the presence of segregated schools was unsightly, deleterious, and economically disadvantageous.

Many organizations and individuals of differing political persuasions toiled mightily to eradicate the most visible element of Indianapolis's commitment to segregation. But the solid front was a mere facade, which crumbled easily when more difficult issues tested its strength. Ransom and Richardson had their law, but it would prove ineffective in the face of creative opposition. Judge Niblack and the Citizens Committee would continue to be a worthy and persistent opponent. Thurgood Marshall's suggestion to let the courts intervene appeared more appealing and increasingly necessary as a well-choreographed dance involving integrationists and obstructionists continued.

For many, including the influential Eugene Pulliam, as long as the 1949 law removed the stigma of a segregated school system from the city's midst, actual reform was of little concern. As school integrationists found in other parts of the United States after *Brown* v. *Board of Education* (1954), having a law to end desegregation was far different from actual integration. African American pursuit of a reform law was a good and reasonable strategy, but the law did not dictate procedure. The school board, whose composition was largely unchanged after the 1949 law, proved to be as adept at forestalling integration as it had been at parrying community activists.

The school board's approval of Superintendent Stinebaugh's plans for a very gradual integration of the school system initiated the first step in the delay. Under Stinebaugh's plan, schoolchildren entering kindergarten or the first grade could enroll in the school nearest their home. The plan was gradual because Stinebaugh advocated a year-by-year integration plan. High school registration was dictated by two separate guidelines also found in Stinebaugh's proposal. Students would attend the high school where their elementary school directed them prior to the 1949 law. If the distance of that high school from the student's home was greater than two miles, then the school board would entertain appeals for a change. Clearly, the plan would maintain segregation unless aggrieved students and their families undertook special efforts. Further, no white students were assigned to Crispus Attucks, and there would not be a white student so assigned until 1968.[58]

Interpretations of desegregation efforts varied greatly. By 1953, the school board announced desegregation complete, at which time about two-thirds of the city's student population attended integrated schools. School administrators boasted that desegregation had occurred two years earlier than the date mandated by the 1949 law. In so boasting, they would be truthful but not entirely accurate. Although 67 percent of the student population attended schools not solely inhabited by children of one race, several schools were hardly integrated. Whites were minorities in only four schools, and of those four, two had only one white student. Two other schools had only one black student. The *Indianapolis Times* was so emboldened by the Indianapolis desegregation efforts that they felt obliged to counsel southern states to accept desegregation with little worry. Indianapolis had proven that desegregation, if done correctly, could be attained peacefully. The *Indianapolis News* reported no "major upheavals" associated with desegregation. Gradualism seemed to be the necessary ingredient for the harmonious mixing of races within a schoolroom setting.[59]

Members of the black community did not share the school board's opinion regarding the completion of desegregation. An investigation conducted by the local NAACP branch determined that the school board continued to "have colored schools with colored teachers and white schools with white teachers indefinitely—regardless of the letter and spirit of the law." School personnel records substantiated the NAACP's findings. In the year prior to the report, the school system appointed sixty-seven new white teachers to fill "anticipated vacancies"; at the same time the school system dismissed two black teachers because there were "no vacancies." The *Recorder* questioned the intentions of the board with reference to these appointments and dismissals. It also particularly complained that the school board was perpetuating segregation through gerrymandered districts and pupil assignments.[60]

The largest and most damning evidence lodged against the school board was the continued segregation of Crispus Attucks High School. Even Attucks's state championships in basketball (1955 and 1956), no trivial event in basketball-crazed Indiana, brought no relief from segregation. Statements issued by the school board failed to adequately explain the existence of a black-only high school. White students within Attucks's district continued to be assigned either to Manual or Shortridge High Schools. Attucks's exclusively black student body reaffirmed opponents' claims that segregation was alive and well in Indianapolis schools.[61]

Although criticism from the *Recorder* and other organizations continued unabated throughout the decade, it was not until 1959 that the League of Women Voters and the Indianapolis Council of Parents and Teachers mounted an effective challenge to the Citizens Committee. Judge Niblack remained the driving force behind the committee, and the organization continued its practice of controlling nominations for the school board. While the League of Women Voters did not directly challenge the committee's nominating practices or segregationist policies, it did see both issues as part of a larger problem of undemocratic and non-representative behavior. The League of Women Voters studied fifty cities to determine a more effective and representative way to elect school boards. In presenting their recommendations to the Citizens Committee, they hoped to help the committee achieve its stated goal of providing qualified nominees. Judge Niblack did not welcome this uninvited intrusion and told representatives of the League of Women Voters that they were out of order.[62]

Adele Thomas, president of the League of Women Voters, maintained that the League of Women Voters' recommendations did not intend to threaten the Citizens Committee's domain. Although that may not have been the League's intent, its recommendations did in fact threaten the committee because the League of Women Voters wanted to bring into public light what the Citizens Committee had long done privately. The League of Women Voters offered six recommendations for the Committee's consideration: (1) Make public the specific bylaws used by the committee; (2) provide a clear statement of committee purposes, duties, and functions; (3) create a membership policy that specified how members are obtained and how long each member is to serve; (4) formulate a stronger statement on the non-partisan character of the committee along with a provision that no elected official could serve on the executive committee; (5) implement a definite system of selection with stated terms for officers and rotation of membership on the executive board; and (6) encourage greater membership participation in decisions of the committee.[63] Thomas may have thought that the recommendations were innocuous and non-threatening, but in essence her organization's efforts to demystify the nomination process attacked the heart of the Citizens Committee's strength. Niblack's power rested in part on his freedom to act without interference from any outside monitoring agency. However, in summarily dismissing the League's proposals, the committee alienated a group that was well respected in the community.[64]

A little more than ten years after the last successful interracial coalition fought for a desegregation law, another organization, the Committee for Better Schools (CBS), was poised to do battle with the Citizens Committee. Following a decade of repeated insults by the school board that culminated in the rejection of the League of Women Voters proposal, CBS offered a challenge to the Citizens Committee. The CBS's membership included more than two hundred Indianapolis residents drawn from a wide range of organizations such as the NAACP, church and labor groups, the Mayor's Commission on Human Rights, and the League of Women Voters. A few former members of the Citizens Committee, critical of its exclusiveness, had also joined the CBS. Charges of exclusiveness could hardly be leveled against the Committee for Better Schools, as anyone could join the group by paying the $1 membership fee. The CBS's self-stated purpose was "to provide the citizens of Indianapolis an opportunity to participate, in a democratic manner, in the nomination and election of the School Commissioners."[65]

Perhaps coincidentally, the day after the organizational meeting of the CBS, Dr. Herman Shibler resigned as superintendent of schools. Shibler enjoyed warm support from the black community because his efforts at integration were consistent and evenhanded. Most gratifying had been his practice of listening to suggestions from the community. The *Recorder* absolved Shibler from any blame in the slow movement toward integration and instead placed full responsibility on the school board that had worked to block and stall Shibler's efforts. Shibler intimated to *Recorder* staffers that he had been told to resign or be fired. He chose the former and negotiated a settlement that extended his salary for six months after resignation.[66]

That Shibler's resignation under duress occurred almost simultaneously with the CBS's creation presaged a bitter fall campaign season. While the CBS did not include provisions for integration of either students or teachers, the *Recorder* endorsed its commitment to representation, democracy, and fairness.[67] The CBS pledged to keep politics out of school administration and to be influenced solely by the needs of the community. Its openness, especially in membership, made it ripe for attack by the Citizens Committee. Niblack's group chastised the CBS for being under the influence of labor unions, the Indiana Civil Liberties Union, the NAACP, and other "interest groups."[68]

Identification with labor unions became a major theme late in the campaign, with both the *Star* and *News* carrying bold headlines linking CBS candidates to labor unions.[69] Such negative publicity had its effect. City residents seemed to agree with the *Star* and the *News:* if CBS candidates were victorious, teachers would soon become unionized. On November 4, 1959, Citizens Committee candidates again swept the election.[70]

Again, an attempt to effect change through the placing of sympathetic members on the school board had failed. It is true that organized labor and the Parent Teacher Association (PTA), an organization long viewed with suspicion by the Citizens Committee, openly supported the CBS. It is unclear whether the CBS would have acted promptly to erase segregation in Indianapolis's public schools. It is likely, however, that continued segregation would not have been palatable to a group as inclusive as the CBS. Nevertheless, the 1959 election did indicate that most of the electorate was happy with the stewardship provided by Citizens Committee candidates and was unwilling to change the composition or the direction of the school board. Having yet again failed at the ballot box, reformers in the black community now looked to the federal government and courts to bring about long-desired changes.

During the early years of the 1960s there was much activity in the capital city in the areas of housing and labor. One historian has argued that African American communities tended to concentrate their protest efforts, resulting in significant time gaps between reform undertakings as vocal leaders hopscotched from one crisis to another. Their history in Indianapolis fits this pattern. The black community faced significant issues other than school segregation, and a sometimes overburdened African American community, as we shall see, confronted those. While the fight for a quality school system waxed and waned, many combatants were also fighting for better housing and representation on community policy-making boards. Notwithstanding continued protests and challenges, such as a successful effort to upgrade Crispus Attucks High School's facilities, the pace of school desegregation did not quicken until the United States Department of Justice got involved.[71] In 1965, Andrew Ramsey, president of the NAACP state conference, a teacher at Attucks, and an ardent supporter of African American civil rights efforts, wrote to John Gardner, Secretary of Health, Education, and Welfare (HEW), requesting a federal investigation of discrimination in the assignment of teachers.[72]

Entrance by the federal government should have been expected. In 1963, a United States Civil Rights Commission reported that desegregation efforts in Indianapolis were "minimal."[73] As is customary, it was some time before the federal government acted on its own finding. It was 1968 before the Civil Rights Division of the Department of Justice directed the Indianapolis school board to take voluntary steps to alleviate Fourteenth Amendment violations. The Justice Department found fault with the school board's practice of assigning faculty members based on race and the perpetuation of segregated elementary and secondary schools. Mark Gray, president of the Board of School Commissioners, responded to the Justice Department request by asserting Indianapolis's laudable efforts and defending the concept of "neighborhood schools."[74] Despite the assertion that there was "no hint of segregation" in the assignment of pupils or teachers, school officials did take halting steps to speed the process of desegregation. But their efforts insulted African Americans who were growing tired of stalling actions, and they angered whites who resented federal intervention.[75]

The neighborhood school controversy became the fulcrum of the ensuing legal debate. As residential segregation became more solidified, it was possible to maintain a race-neutral assignment policy while simultaneously preserving segregated schools. The Justice Department did not agree that the Indianapolis school board had done all in its power to alleviate segregation; rather, they contended that the school board gerrymandered school districts in an effort to maintain segregated schools. In the years since the 1949 school desegregation law went into effect, Indianapolis had had more than 360 boundary changes. Black schools had new additions that allowed them to house an even greater number of students rather than redirect students to white schools, and new high school construction took place on the outskirts of town, the very areas where blacks were least likely to live. In 1968, the Justice Department filed suit in federal court seeking jurist-mandated integration.[76]

Almost simultaneously, and perhaps not coincidentally, Mayor Dick Lugar was seeking adoption of Unified Government (Unigov), a complicated merger of city and county government functions. Lugar had begun his political career with a stint on the school board in the early 1960s. Considered a moderate because of his views concerning acceptance of federal funds, Lugar hailed Unigov as a more economical and efficient way to run a city. Schools played an important part in Unigov's plan and it was likely that Lugar's experience on the school board allowed him to witness how determined whites were to keep the races separate in the schools. When Unigov was enacted, school corporations maintained their own autonomy, allowing suburban communities to remain in sole control of educational policy. The state authorized the implementation of Unigov in 1969, just as the Justice Department was pressuring for a court solution to entrenched educational segregation.

The Department of Health, Education, and Welfare (HEW) did not wait for the courts. In the late spring of 1969, HEW recommended that students from predominantly black elementary schools be grouped with students from predominantly white elementary schools in an effort to desegregate all affected schools. Students at Attucks, the report continued, should be transferred and new districts drawn to change the feeder schools supplying students to the still all-black high school. HEW adroitly avoided the issue of busing, a factor that was already a lightning rod for public dissent.[77]

Disregarding strong black community support, the school board unanimously rejected HEW's recommendations.[78] Instead, the school board promised to create a representative community committee to examine alternate plans to achieve integration and academic excellence. African American groups and individuals were not inactive or silent during the deliberations concerning desegregation; however, no one plan won unanimous support. There were four suggestions proffered for Attucks: eradication, integration, adoption of a special high school curriculum (similar to a present-day magnet school), or the creation of a junior college. The various plans represented the many fractures existing within the black community by 1969. Before the 1960s, most important organizations, FAC, Flanner House, and the YMCA, were primarily under local control and relatively moderate. By 1969, however, CORE, SNCC, the Black Panthers, and the Urban League all had chapters in Indianapolis, and their presence brought greater diversity to African American protest. In 1963, Andrew Ramsey had warned the white community that corrective measures in race relations should be undertaken before problems erupted. Essentially, Ramsey was urging Indianapolis to clean up its act before outsiders instigated "situations over which we have no control."[79]

African Americans may not have agreed on one plan for Attucks, but they did agree on one solution to desegregation. If busing was to occur, not a prospect eagerly anticipated by any group, it would have to involve the busing of both white and black children. Having exhausted all reasonable attempts, African Americans now had only the court to turn to for redress. Long after Thurgood Marshall's efforts in *Brown* v. *Board of Education* (1954) had seemingly settled the question of school segregation, Indianapolis began its court case on school desegregation.

Pursuant to the Civil Rights Act of 1964, the Department of Justice filed suit against the Board of School Commissioners; George F. Ostheimer, superintendent of schools; Mark W. Gray, president of the Board of School Commissioners; and the other six members of the Board of School Commissioners. The Justice Department charged the defendants with unlawful racial discrimination by segregating students on the basis of race, by assigning faculty and staff members on the basis of race, and by constructing and maintaining Crispus Attucks High School as a segregated school.[80] United States District Judge S. Hugh Dillin was assigned the case. By the time the case was finally resolved twenty years later, the original cast of plaintiffs and defendants had completely changed. Additional parties had attempted to become either defendants or plaintiffs, but were rebuked. Of the original participants, only Judge Dillin remained. Even the Board of School Commissioners, which was among the original defendants, changed its legal representation a number of times during the case.

A summary of the litigation provides some insight into the core issues of the case. Judge Dillin quickly and consistently found the Indianapolis Public

Schools guilty of operating a segregated school system. Dillin found the school board's actions constituted de jure segregation, especially their construction of new facilities and manipulation of school district boundaries. He also found the state of Indiana culpable. The Department of Public Instruction had sanctioned the building of new schools that perpetuated segregation. But the most contentious issue was Unigov. Dillin found that Unigov, through its provisions abdicating authority over suburban schools, helped to continue segregation. Lawyers for the plaintiffs tried unsuccessfully to get a favorable ruling on the constitutionality of Unigov. At various times throughout the case, Judge Dillin pleaded with concerned parties to work out a mutually acceptable settlement. The defendants met each supplication with inaction. They opted to appeal virtually every judicial decision and in so doing effectively delayed school desegregation until the 1980s.

John Moss and John Ward represented the African American plaintiffs. Moss was a member of a three-person law firm, and Ward was a sole practitioner. The Justice Department remained a plaintiff in the case, but as Judge Dillin ordered an interdistrict remedy, one in which city schools and suburban schools participated fully in the desegregation plan, Justice Department lawyers became increasingly silent. At one trial, the Justice Department called no witnesses. The plaintiffs often faced more than twenty lawyers at a time, each ably supported by large law firms. The Justice Department had abandoned the plaintiffs because the policy of the Richard Nixon administration was to maintain suburban community autonomy, a departure from his predecessor, President Lyndon B. Johnson. In the Indianapolis case, Justice Department attorneys eventually sided with the defendants in recommending an intrasystem desegregation plan. In a bizarre twist, the Justice Department had come to side with their original opponents.[81]

Judge Dillin found that interdistrict cooperation was the only solution for Indianapolis. If only schools within Indianapolis were subject to desegregation, Dillin feared white families would rush to the suburbs, thereby causing a re-segregation of city schools. The only remedy to such a scenario was to include suburban schools. The "tipping point," that elusive figure where blacks would be tolerated at a majority white school without causing white flight, fluctuated wildly. Dillin initially thought the figure, based on testimony by sociologists and educators, was around 40 percent. By 1976, Dillin had lowered that figure to 15 percent. He ordered black students in Indianapolis from grades one through nine transferred to each of the suburban school districts in such numbers as would cause the total enrollment of each suburban school to approximate 15 percent black students. Of course, the defendant schools appealed Judge Dillin's ruling.[82]

Indianapolis fought school desegregation with a ferocity rarely matched by any other northern city. Citizens wrote harsh words in the press, and Judge

Dillin had to survive two impeachment attempts. In the end, only one tenet of the original case, the assignment of teachers on a race-neutral basis, had been settled and implemented. To some, Judge Dillin was a villain, to others a hero, and at times he was surely the most despised man in Indianapolis. But it was the consistent pressure applied by the black community that proved to be the most compelling force. Long after his own children had finished their schooling, Arthur Boone fought to allow black children to go to appropriate schools. He was not alone. The NAACP and concerned citizens did not abandon the cause. Their style of protest preserved the peace and relatively harmonious race relations, but it failed to achieve timely, effective change. Victory proved to be elusive as the city of Indianapolis, through both legal and extralegal means, struggled to maintain a dual system based on racial placement of students. By the time Dillin reached his decision, there was little doubt that the African American and white communities had become adversaries. The initial lawyers, Robert Lee Brokenburr and F. B. Ransom, models of public decorum, and many others had tirelessly fought to achieve two goals that proved incongruent: they had tried to eradicate segregated schools while remaining collegial with their white counterparts. They had tried all of the measures of civil discourse, petition, coalition building, and voting, before resorting to the last recourse offered them. In the end, the successors to Brokenburr and Ransom could not achieve either of the initial goals, and perhaps they no longer concerned themselves with the impact of their action on the level of collegiality.

3

"We Were Always Fighting the Housing Battle"

African American Housing in Indianapolis

"I want to make a living and get out of this old dump. I want a decent house for my kids."

"Well, we like it here better than Georgia. We at least live better."[1]

Housing segregation is not merely an act of racism or a consequence of home-owners' sensitivity to the market value of their homes. While each explanation is reasonable, this study will show that the size of the African American population determined the level of housing discrimination in Indianapolis. As the percentage of African Americans in the city's population grew, attempts to sequester African Americans increased.[2] Housing issues posed some of the most complex and intractable problems for Indianapolis's African American community. The homes African Americans most often inhabited immediately before and after World War II were below standard and sometimes lacked the most basic amenities like plumbing and electricity. However, throughout much of the twentieth century, one constant remained: in an attempt to improve their housing stock and dispersal throughout the city, African Americans fought avaricious landlords, intransigent and greedy realtors, and those ideologically opposed to federal aid. Unfortunately, however, African Americans never effectively marshaled their numeric strength into successful political agitation.

An elemental question for the examination of any protest effort is: What issues or insults will a group fight over and how forcefully will they engage in the struggle? Complicating things immeasurably was the fact that throughout much of the twentieth century, the home ownership rate for African Americans in Indianapolis was greater than that of any other African American community in the north. Consequently, while African Americans endured housing inadequacies, they were also knowledgeable of their enviable position. African Americans living in the infamous crowded conditions found on

Chicago's south side could look enviously at Indianapolis's housing stock. What follows, therefore, is not solely an exploration of African American protest or the discriminatory practices African Americans encountered. These two elements conflicted, spurred on by larger forces such as the ideological pursuit for free enterprise, economic advantage for specific groups, and political party positioning. The battle lines were neighborhood construction, housing availability, and condition. But as in so many battles, the causes of the conflict were removed from the battle's center. African Americans continually confronted the same question: How much and what type of protest would prove effective while not costing previously won gains? Their actions in response to that question changed over time; their protest efforts were as flexible as the challenges they faced.

As with educational segregation, African Americans encountered the significant impediment caused by at-large voting. Without ward representation, local political leaders did not fight for open housing because it brought them no political advantage and possibly meant significant costs. Those advocating free enterprise and property rights hampered integration efforts. These ideologies took root in the local political economy, and open housing advocates could not rely on consistent support from either political party. Never too far below the surface was the recognition that local real estate interests profited from a system that bifurcated the housing stock along racial lines. Consequently, open housing advocates were much more successful in gaining state initiatives than in securing local reform. While white reaction to the growing African American population began the process of segregation, the profits that property owners and realtors gained from the bifurcated housing market fueled its continuation. But African Americans never conceded to residential segregation, and they fought discriminatory practices in the fashion consistent with the community's protest efforts. When negotiations faltered or failed, African Americans resorted to creative means to better the housing options available to them. Their creative and labor-intensive attempts to surmount their housing realities were laudable, but they may have unintentionally added to housing inequality. It would be incorrect to say that African Americans were complicit in creating Indianapolis's segregated condition. It is more accurate to argue that their protest strategies were inconsistent, often contradictory, and allowed Jim Crow housing to flourish in the capital city.

As the twentieth century progressed, Indianapolis mirrored the experience of some of its better-known northern neighbors and increasingly sequestered its African American population within single-race neighborhoods.[3] Only their relatively large numbers mitigated the extent to which they were clustered in this manner.[4] There were simply too many African Americans in Indianapolis to squeeze into one neighborhood. By 1910, 9.3 percent of the city's total population was African American, the highest percentage of any city north of the Ohio River. Consequently, three distinct, non-contiguous African American neighborhoods formed. The oldest, along the canal directly northwest of downtown and dubbed Pat Ward's Bottoms or the Bottoms, was established during and after the Civil War. The second was north of the Bottoms along present-day Martin Luther King Boulevard. The youngest neighborhood was on the east side, near Douglas Park, in present-day Brightwood. It was peopled during the early decades when industry rapidly expanded in Indianapolis.[5]

During the period that Indianapolis established itself as an industrial city of the first order, there was seemingly little concern about the growing African American presence in the city. Perhaps city boosters were too excited over the scarcity of foreigners to take note of the growing black population. The Indianapolis establishment went so far as to herald the city's demographics in publicity material as "this 100 percent American town" and "the capital of the land of opportunity." The Commercial Club sang the loudest praise of the city's American homogeneity, declaring in 1910, "There is almost a total absence of the foreign floating element," a factor, they further argued, which explained why tenements and violence were virtually unknown in the city. Perhaps because of the relative scarcity of foreigners, ethnic isolation was not as pronounced in Indianapolis as it was in some of the larger cities in the North.[6] But the relative quiet that had accompanied previous African American migration changed after World War I, when migration continued and whites began to take increasing notice of the growing African American population. By 1920, the black population of Indianapolis had grown to 34,678 (11 percent of the city's population). The larger black population strained the existing housing and labor market, and whites reacted to the increased African American presence with demands for heightened segregation, especially in public accommodations and public schools.[7]

The African Americans who had resided in the city for decades recognized the increased segregation but did not fight forcefully to withstand the onslaught. In adjusting to discrimination, Indianapolis's African Americans recognized they were sacrificing certain basic rights of citizenship. An editorial in the *Indianapolis Freeman*, a weekly newspaper with a primarily African American readership, noted:

> We have learned to forego some rights that are common, and because we know the price. We would gain but little in a way if certain places were thrown open to us. We have not insisted that hotels should entertain our race, or the theaters, rights that are clearly ours.[8]

The editorial staff of the influential *Freeman* counseled its readers to concede certain rights, but they also strongly urged African Americans to retain the right to live where they chose.[9] African Americans, as represented by the *Freeman*, conceded certain public limitations, but found that the location of their home was a private decision and that residents should be allowed to choose where they were to live, limited only by desire and ability to pay.[10]

When African Americans did move into neighborhoods exclusively inhabited by whites, their neighbors often tried to harass them into leaving. A favorite practice of the Capitol Avenue Protective Association, a group that functioned as a self-selected collective of residents living near Capitol Avenue interested in preserving the area's homogeneity, was the construction of "spite" fences. Whites constructed high walls surrounding the property of any black family who moved into the neighborhood. The walls surrounded three sides of the "intruder's" property. Some methods of harassment were not so benign. A black family that moved into a white neighborhood in 1924 survived a hand grenade thrown through their window. After the incident, handbills appeared in surrounding neighborhoods asking, "DO YOU WANT A NIGGER FOR A NEIGHBOR?" By custom, a "White Supremacy Dead Line" existed at 27th Street, above which no African Americans were allowed to rent or purchase homes. The Mapleton Civic Association, an organization that included prominent businessmen among its members, codified its members' feelings in a statement of aims: "One of our chief concerns is to prevent members of the colored race from moving into our midst, thereby depreciating property values fifty per cent, or more." Members pledged not to sell or rent property to anyone except a white person, and they fulfilled their mission. The *Freeman* reported that for years no African Americans moved into the Mapleton area.[11]

Indianapolis residents were unusually persistent in their desire to stay put. Regardless of race or ethnicity, citizens typically remained in one neighborhood for most of their lives. Perhaps people accepted limited geographic mobility because they were happy in their neighborhoods. One of Indianapolis's nicknames was "the city of homes," and the claim was no hollow cliché. There was a high level of home ownership in Indianapolis throughout much of the twentieth century. Furthermore, Indianapolis residents, both black and white, lived with fewer occupants per dwelling on average than did residents of Chicago, Cincinnati, Louisville, or Columbus, Ohio, during the same period.[12]

The frequency with which Indianapolis male heads of household left the city was apparently unrelated to race, with African Americans only slightly more prone to move than whites. In establishing this pattern, Indianapolis's African American citizens resembled their southern counterparts more than they did their northern neighbors. During a similar period, persistence rates for African Americans in Birmingham, Alabama, and Atlanta, Georgia, were higher than those for whites. Neither whites nor African Americans moved frequently or over great distances, but to accept the notion that race had little to do with geographic mobility after 1920 would require ignoring too many factors. By the mid-1920s, African Americans already faced a severe housing shortage. Redlining (so named because of realtors' penchant for drawing a red line on a map around the area inhabited by African Americans), hostile white reactions, and inferior housing combined to create a black housing shortage. Historian Emma Lou Thornbrough wrote of the 1920s that "[b]arred by white prejudice, which was reinforced by policies of white Realtors, African Americans were confined to clearly recognizable 'colored neighborhoods.'"[13] African Americans did not move because there was nowhere in the city for them to go.

The limited mobility afforded African Americans was graphically reflected by the Home Owners' Loan Corporation's residential security map and street index, which was produced under the direction of the Federal Home Loan Bank Board. The purpose of the map was to portray graphically the trend of desirability in neighborhoods from a residential viewpoint. Although bureaucrats in Washington, D.C., conducted the survey, local real estate brokers and mortgage lenders were consulted to assure accuracy. Financial lenders were in a position to assess the quality of neighborhoods because their reluctance to provide financing for purchase or renovation of existing homes effectively sealed a neighborhood's fate.

The map classified neighborhoods according to four categories. The letters A, B, C, and D represented neighborhoods based on the following characteristics: percentage of home ownership; age and type of building; economic stability of the area; social status of the population; sufficiency of public utilities; accessibility of schools, churches, and business centers; transportation methods; topography of the area; and the restrictions set up to protect the neighborhood. The price of the homes was not a guiding factor. The A areas were the "hot spots." In nearly every instance, they were new construction in well-planned sections of the city, homogeneous, and in demand as residential locations irrespective of economic cycles. The B areas, as a rule, were almost completely developed, established neighborhoods that were nearly completely homogeneous. The C areas were characterized by structure, age, obsolescence, expiring restrictions or lack of them, infiltration of a lower-grade population, the presence of influences that increased sales resistance, such as poor transportation, insufficient utilities, and poor maintenance of homes, and, not coincidentally, lack of homogeneity. The D areas were similar to the C areas except that the transition had already occurred and the negative influences were entrenched.[14]

Not surprisingly, given the qualifier of homogeneity, no African Americans lived in the A areas. Only two black families lived in one of the seventeen areas in Indianapolis categorized as B. Therefore, only two African American families resided in neighborhoods deemed still desirable. Most C areas had a few African Americans, but no neighborhood so designated had more than 3 percent of African Americans in its population. African Americans dominated the D areas. In one blighted neighborhood, catalogued as D-25, African Americans made up 90 percent of the population. Class distinctions were noted among the black community in the survey. Adjacent to D-25 was area D-27, which was bounded on the north by 30th Street and on the south by 24th Street. According to the Home Owners' Loan Corporation, this area was home to the "better class of Negroes, including teachers, doctors, etc., many of whom are home-owners. Local lending institutions are satisfied to make loans to people in this class in this neighborhood."[15] The recognition of class differences did not mitigate the Home Owners' Loan Corporation's assessment; the area housing the "better class" of African Americans was still catalogued as D.

Despite restrictions in housing and employment, the black population of Indianapolis continued to grow. By 1930, African Americans constituted almost 12 percent of the Indianapolis population, compared to 4.1 percent of the Chicago population at the time.[16] At the time of the Great Depression, the black population had increased 175 percent in thirty years, from 15,931 in 1900 to nearly 44,000 in 1930. The city's industrial base and close proximity to southern states, as well as the significant number of African Americans already living in the city, continued to lure African Americans to Indianapolis. However, a growing population restricted to a finite area inevitably encountered problems. The larger population altered the fragile symbiosis between white and black residents, and it became increasingly common for black and white citizens to compete for housing within the same ward. The boundaries were not as well demarcated as those found in a census or a map, but citizens were well aware of who belonged in their neighborhood and where each belonged.

In 1926, the Indianapolis City Council passed an ordinance that was intended to "promote good order and general welfare" through the separation of white and black residential communities. The measure created sanctions against whites moving into a "portion of the municipality inhabited principally by Negroes" or African Americans establishing residence in a "white community," except with the written consent of a majority of the opposite race inhabiting the neighborhood. The council's bold attempt to maintain racially segregated neighborhoods was especially egregious because the ordinance was passed after the United States Supreme Court had ruled a similar Louisville law unconstitutional in 1917.[17] Ordinance supporters on the council thought Indianapolis could avoid the court's censure because their ordinance did not expressly prohibit the sale of property or give any particular advantage to members of either race; it merely prohibited occupancy. The court failed to see the distinction and summarily struck down the Indianapolis ordinance, but its presence was not really needed because real estate agents refused to show African Americans property outside of designated areas.[18]

By the time of the Great Depression, the efforts of real estate agents had borne fruit. African Americans were increasingly sequestered within the three distinct neighborhoods defined earlier, resulting in a severe housing shortage. Regardless of their economic status, African Americans looking for housing faced overcrowding, dilapidation, health hazards, and overpricing. In 1939, Flanner House hosted a symposium to discuss the condition of the black community in Indianapolis. The attendees insisted that

> Wholesome housing and living simply cannot be reduced to a statistic. Too many qualitative and suggestive factors are involved. . . . The areas in which Negroes live are those made vacant by population pressure, areas of transition, which are in most cases undesirable for residential purposes, with high rent values, but worn out dwellings. Most dwellings have depreciated considerably. Perhaps the factor which conditions Negro housing to an even greater degree than those mentioned above is the fact that the Negro simply cannot afford to pay for much better housing because of the economic status of the group.[19]

Flanner House's cautious statement let real estate interests and segregation proponents off the hook. Instead of highlighting the limitations placed on prospective African American homeowners and renters, conference delegates chose to emphasize the economic condition of the African American community. Moreover, Flanner House easily could have echoed the findings of the Federal Housing Administration and the Indiana Real Estate Association, both of which had issued statements decrying the scarcity of low-income housing in Indiana.[20]

In the seven years following World War II, no fewer than three major studies documented the housing crisis among African Americans. The studies offered varying solutions. In 1946, Flanner House published a study of 454 African American households in Pat Ward's Bottoms. The purpose of the study was to give the Indianapolis Redevelopment Commission a realistic assessment of the housing situation for a sample group of African Americans. Flanner House hoped their study would help the commission more ably redevelop and aid an area largely inhabited by African Americans. After studying the report, city leaders decided that the best redevelopment of the area was to demolish all existing structures.[21]

At the same time, the Metropolitan Housing Commission conducted a study on the value and availability of housing in Indianapolis. The commission found housing shortages, which they expected, but were dismayed to learn that of the nearly 4,000 available units, approximately 1,600 were substandard. So, while the Redevelopment Commission recommended the destruction of an African American neighborhood where homes were occupied, another agency highlighted the inadequate housing supply. Eugenia Hollis, in her exhaustive examination of seventeen housing studies conducted on the Indianapolis community, concluded:

> The needs of the Negro group are the most acute. The general housing shortage is aggravated for this group by the existence of restrictive covenants and discrimination in renting or selling to them. Furthermore, the proportion of families renting homes is higher among Negroes than among whites, a situation that

will probably continue since there is no basis for assuming that the economic conditions of the Negroes have changed materially during the war period. The method by which low cost housing on a rental basis for the Negro group may be provided is one of the major problems to be faced in any planning for improvement of housing in Indianapolis.[22]

In 1952, The Church Federation of Indianapolis, an ecumenical and interracial organization begun in 1908, sponsored a clinic to analyze the problems of race relations in the city and to develop solutions to overcome those problems. Their findings confirmed those expressed by Eugenia Hollis. At the conclusion of the clinic, the Church Federation reported that racism was the most important factor shaping African American housing: "Housing congestion is more acute among Negroes than among other minority groups because race prejudice provides an artificial check to their expansion into new areas." They especially decried the existence of "racial restrictive covenants," the practice of including in contracts of sale a provision prohibiting African Americans from buying property.[23]

In effect, every sizable organization that examined the housing situation in Indianapolis echoed what African Americans had said for decades, namely, that the city needed immediate and bountiful new housing construction, and the enforcement of laws prohibiting racial restrictions in housing contracts. No person or organization could reasonably contend that adequate housing existed, yet while a crisis was certainly underway, there was little agreement on appropriate solutions. For the next thirty years, culminating during Lyndon B. Johnson's presidency, local, state, and national leaders all tried their hand at alleviating the housing shortage, with varying degrees of success. The federal government advocated public housing, which was never popular with Indianapolis officials. Flanner House and the city collaborated on a bold self-help program that oversaw the construction of quality homes, but not in too great a number. The NAACP, in cooperation with other organizations, fought for local legislation that would enforce open housing. Finally, it was left to private citizens to work through the logjam themselves with cooperation and compromise, the very qualities in short supply earlier in the century.

The first significant attempt to ease the shortage began during the Great Depression. Federal officials hoped they could ease the housing shortage by constructing Lockefield Gardens, a 784-unit public housing complex. Not coincidentally, they could also use public housing to help maintain racially separate neighborhoods. Begun in 1934 by the Housing Division of the Federal Emergency Administration of Public Works and the Advisory Committee on Housing of Indianapolis, Lockefield Gardens was located on Indiana Avenue, near the center of Indianapolis's oldest African American neighborhood and one of the most blighted areas in the city.

The decision to create federally sponsored public housing did not come about without significant worry and objection from Indianapolis real estate concerns. Homebuilders and the Indianapolis Real Estate Board were concerned that construction of public housing would lead to vacancies in privately owned rental properties. Lionel F. Artis, the African American manager of Lockefield Gardens, tried to reassure private landlords that Lockefield's presence would not cause a housing glut. He reminded all interested parties that the housing crisis was severe: "Our records show that between 200 and 300 families accepted as tenants for Lockefield are now doubled-up with other families. . . . Most of the houses to be deserted by many families are far below standard." Despite Artis's claims, private interests, led by the Indianapolis Real Estate Board and local contractors, continued to challenge any initiative to provide low-cost public housing. Their efforts were well rewarded. The housing shortage that profited landlords and promoted high rents for substandard dwellings continued to exist for decades.[24]

Local housing profiteers were unable to stop the construction of Lockefield Gardens. It was difficult for even the most ardent private housing advocate to argue that the system adequately met citizen needs. When construction of Lockefield Gardens was completed in 1937, the average African American dwelling in Indianapolis lacked modern plumbing and electricity. Most housing was overcrowded and judged substandard by an evaluative team working for the Work Projects Administration. A 1939 Flanner House survey found the area immediately north-northwest of downtown, which was heavily populated by African Americans, to be one of the most unsightly, unsanitary, and deteriorated sectors in the city. Nathan Straus, former United States Housing Administrator, outpaced the authors of the Flanner House report when he alleged that the area was "the worst Negro slum in America."[25]

In present-day parlance, the people who inhabited the area were the "working poor." Most of the families had two wage earners. A study conducted in 1945 found that the median weekly income during World War II was $26.70 per family. On average, families paid $13 a month for rent. A full 50 percent of the homes did not have a yard; of the remaining, 21.8 percent had poorly maintained yards. But the deterioration probably reflected landlord neglect more than occupant negligence, for 80 percent of the families in the survey rented their homes. A full 60.5 percent of the families surveyed had attempted to secure better housing but were unable to relocate. Faced with a public housing system that was clearly overwhelmed, and blocked from moving into areas where housing was available, African Americans were effectively bottled up.[26]

The federal government constructed Lockefield Gardens for the purpose of housing low-income African Americans. Lockefield Gardens' promotional literature heralded the site as "a modern low rent housing project developed in a residential area occupied by negro families."[27] The housing unit reserved for whites was Tyndall Towne, completed in 1946. Unlike Lockefield Gardens, Tyndall Towne's four units (738 apartments) were located at four separate sites around the city, using a scattered site approach familiar and popular with present-day public housing advocates. In its design and site plan, Lockefield Gardens was the model for public housing projects across the United States. Developers hoped to provide a setting where low-income families could live in decent, safe, sanitary, spacious dwellings. But by placing all the units at one location, the federal government merely mimicked the existing housing segregation already prevalent in Indianapolis.

The federal government encouraged tenants to participate in the management of the complex through the Tenant's Council, a policy-making and legislative body. Lockefield Gardens was simply beautiful. Wilma Green, a longtime Indianapolis resident recalled, "Lockefield Gardens . . . drew a lot of people to the area. In those days—before it became public housing [*sic*]—Lockefield was a wonderful place to live, and people used to come from all over town to see the beautiful flower trees that bloomed there every year."[28] Evidently, Lockefield was so beautiful that Ms. Green forgot that it began as public housing. Lockefield Gardens was a community rather than simply a collection of residential structures; the plan included an elementary school, a play yard, and ample living space between and behind apartment buildings. Developers believed that children needed space to play and that families needed an area to call their own—a relatively novel idea in the late 1930s. Row houses were placed facing a central mall, or green, which was a large, landscaped area. Designers used only one-fourth of the physical space allocated to the project for the actual buildings, the rest was landscaped.

Designers also paid careful attention to individual apartments, emphasizing comfortable and functional spaces. Each apartment had cross-ventilation to help ward off the effects of hot, humid Indiana summers. Large windows provided ample light, and every apartment had a window with a view of the grounds. Tiling in the bathroom, linoleum floors in the kitchen, and hardwood floors in other rooms were all easy to maintain. Modern plumbing, electric lights, electric stoves, and refrigerators were standard in each apartment.[29] The care given to design and construction imbued residents with a heightened sense of self-esteem and feelings of safety. A chauffeur who moved into Lockefield not long after its construction recalled:

> Mortality rates among our people are high. It is largely because of the living conditions under which we had to exist. But these warm, dry pleasant homes will reduce deaths among us, I think.
>
> Living here gives a man a feeling that he's going somewhere. None of us make much money, but now we have the chance to live decently. It makes a fellow feel like going to work each day when he knows his home is pleasant and not a hovel and an eyesore to return to.[30]

Lionel F. Artis, Lockefield Gardens' property manager, assumed the responsibility for preserving Lockefield's desirability. Artis was legendary for his strict and invasive moral code. Under threat of censure, single women were not allowed to entertain men after a specified hour; tenants whose apartments were unkempt received a visit and a reprimand from Artis; loud parties were not tolerated. Artis sponsored "home beautification" contests, the Dust Bowl basketball tournament (so named because the basketball court for a long time was not paved), and neighborhood beautification weekends. Given the care devoted to apartment design and construction, Lockefield Gardens residents had better housing than a good number of people, tenants and homeowners, black and white, living in private dwellings. Longtime Indianapolis residents recall Lockefield Gardens as the most desirable housing option available to Indianapolis African Americans at the time of its construction.[31]

Apartment rents at Lockefield Gardens were not based on the size of the apartment but on family income. Throughout Lockefield Gardens' existence as a public housing complex, families were required to pay not less than twenty percent of their income for rent, including utilities. The rental rate charged a given family was based on a standard formula of $1 per month rent for each $53 per year net income. Income levels were checked at least once every twelve months, and if the income level did not increase or decrease by $265, rent remained the same. If the change exceeded $265, the rent was adjusted according to the formula. Families whose incomes rose above the limit for continued occupancy received eviction notices and were given six months to find new housing outside of Lockefield Gardens. While they were searching, however, their rent was adjusted to reflect prevailing private rates in the community. Lockefield's rent policy and its strict eviction guidelines for people who exceeded the maximum income level were intended to ensure a steady supply of low-income housing for the community.[32] In effect, however, even families of modest means were compelled to move. Lockefield Gardens' policy dumped families with limited savings onto a housing market in which they were ill-equipped to compete. Instead of buying a home, families that left Lockefield Gardens were frequently forced to rent a dwelling that was inferior and more expensive than their Lockefield Gardens apartment. Displaced tenants fortunate enough to buy a home were often forced to take in boarders or additional family members to help meet the added costs. The wise course of action, undoubtedly employed by some, was to restrict earnings to remain within the income levels proscribed by Lockefield Gardens' rules. The income policy benefited only the private real estate market that absorbed Lockefield Gardens castoffs. Lockefield Gardens' waiting list was long; movement out was never equal to the number of people desiring to relocate there. At the end of 1956, nearly twenty years after it began accepting tenants, more than 694 families remained on its active waiting list.[33]

During World War II, the housing situation worsened. Fort Benjamin Harrison, located on the city's northeast side, was the United States Army's finance center. The Army transferred hundreds of African Americans to Indianapolis to work in the finance center and in so doing introduced a new type of African American migrant to the city. Andrew J. Brown, himself a transplant from Chicago and pastor at St. John's Baptist Church, identified the Fort Benjamin Harrison members as the church's most progressive members.[34] While their jobs were low-grade positions within the federal hierarchy, the salaries African Americans earned at the finance center put them among the more advanced African American wage earners in the city. As they entered the tight housing market that had been artificially constricted by segregationist patterns, they beseeched the Army to intercede.[35]

The federal government recognized the need for additional housing and offered to aid in constructing additional public housing. Indianapolis officials declined the offer. In 1947, when the Indianapolis Committee on Post-War Planning staged a dinner to announce this decision, George Kuhn, the chairman and former president of the Chamber of Commerce, said, "We do not want any recurrence of federal aid, and we won't go begging to Washington for any further extension of the evils of federal aid and federal domination over local units of government."[36] The city council evidently shared Kuhn's viewpoint. In 1949, Mayor Al Feeney established the Indianapolis Housing Authority. During Feeney's administration, the Housing Authority accomplished very little. In 1952, the situation seemed to change during Mayor Al Clark's regime, when the Housing Authority purchased property on which it planned to build additional public housing. But the city council then stymied the Housing Authority's building efforts by passing Ordinance 13, which curtailed the Housing Authority's ability to monitor and evaluate the city's housing stock, censure recalcitrant landlords, and construct public housing, in effect made the Housing Authority a paper lion.[37] Evidently, the city council did not want the mayor's office to control the function of the Housing Authority. The council need not have worried. The United States Housing Authority, which had managed Lockefield Gardens from its inception, strongly urged the Indianapolis Housing Authority to take over management of the local public housing unit.[38] In accord with the city council, Mayor Phillip Bayt, who succeeded Mayor Clark, refused. Thus, it was during the crucial years between 1945 and 1964, when the country was embroiled in issues of race and democracy, that Indianapolis political leaders refused to allow the Housing Authority to enter the fray.

Faced with a shortage of available homes and denied access to homes outside the prescribed neighborhoods, African Americans were forced to adopt a novel approach to meeting their housing needs. Armed with evidence from their 1946 survey, Flanner House officials petitioned the Indianapolis Redevelopment

Commission to purchase land north of Crispus Attucks High School (along present-day Martin Luther King Boulevard) and allow Flanner House to redevelop the area. The Redevelopment Commission then purchased the land for $150,000 and ceded it to Flanner House for development. More likely they ceded it to Cleo Blackburn, Flanner House's director, who by that time had become an integral component in the city's political landscape. Blackburn had solidified Flanner House's position in the community as the conduit between political and economic leaders and the African American population.[39] Flanner House's plan was to provide land and building materials and allow African American clients to provide the labor.

African Americans rushed to sign up for the ambitious and controversial self-help program. For the first time, affordable, new, quality housing was available for purchase. Flanner House could afford to be extremely selective about whom they allowed to participate in the project, and they were. Clarence Wood, Flanner House's bookkeeper and himself a house builder, recalled, "We were thoroughly checked out. They wanted stable families. Only families. A husband and wife and kids if possible. They checked our credit, our time on the job, our work record to see if there were demerits. They wanted to make sure we were solidly employed. They talked to our ministers. They checked police records." The first class of home builders began working in 1950, and they included teachers, police officers, and employees from Lilly Industries. The Flanner House home-building experiment was not a program for low-income African Americans. Those selected to participate in the program were primarily middle-income residents, and, despite the exhaustive and invasive investigation into applicants' backgrounds, hundreds of families remained on the waiting list.[40]

The Flanner House home-building project was the largest self-help housing initiative undertaken in the United States. Its deployment was a direct result of the unwillingness of local leaders to confront discriminatory practices in the city's housing industry. A relatively easy option, one chosen by many cities in the nation, would have been to accept the federal government's offer to construct public housing. Given Indianapolis's refusal to participate in the federal government's program, only local efforts remained as a viable option. Blackburn championed home building because it conformed to the city's desire for local control and also because of the African American community's willingness to participate in an effort—indeed, almost any effort—that promised a cherished outcome. The Flanner House home-building project was a seemingly odd mix of paternalism on behalf of the city's fathers and self-initiative by the African American populace. The city, unwilling to share expenses and control with the federal government, eagerly agreed to provide funds for land clearance; African Americans, halted at every legislative level, were willing to shoulder axe and shovel to construct suitable housing. Above all, the Flanner House project displayed recognition of the political economy at work in the city: local control mixed with a liberal dose of self-help; protest without confrontation.

Not everyone was enamored with Flanner House's effort to ease the housing shortage. In addition to the local construction industry, which oddly did not construct a sufficient number of homes to meet the demand and now saw the volunteer labor as a threat to their livelihood, the national NAACP instructed the local branch to withhold support for the Flanner House home project because the construction of segregated housing violated the integrationist platform of the national office. Flanner House was planning to construct homes in an area that was solidly populated by African Americans. Even more egregious was the displacement of the poor African Americans who lived in the blighted area and who were not guaranteed inclusion in the project. The NAACP urged the local chapter to continue fighting for open housing legislation and for the eradication of redlining and other restrictive devices. Madison S. Jones, special assistant for housing at the NAACP, wrote, "We are not interested in stimulating any interest in all-Negro housing. Our primary purpose and objective is to stimulate interest in integrated housing."[41] The *Indianapolis Recorder* echoed the sentiments of the NAACP but was cognizant of prevailing local conditions. For years, the *Recorder* had championed the cause of open housing, but they recognized that some new housing was better than none. They offered lukewarm support of the building project but lamented the need for such a program.

Despite the counsel of the NAACP, and with a fair bit of local anxiety about the project's long-term success, Flanner House proceeded with the project. Once Flanner House admitted families to the program, the male head of household (only men were allowed to work directly in the construction of homes) worked with the project in his spare time. After putting in a full shift at their principal places of employment, the men changed clothes and went to work building houses. Each man involved in the project helped build his own house and the house of every other man in the project. The floor plans were all the same: 975 square feet, including three bedrooms, one bath, a living room, and kitchen.[42] Flanner House allowed participants to choose one of four available facades. Comprising twenty-eight men, including Clarence Wood, the 1953 group built twenty-eight homes. They drew straws to determine who would get first choice in lot selection and then worked on a number of homes simultaneously. Flanner House sought to get equal numbers of first- and second-shift workers to allow construction from 8:00 A.M. to 9:00 P.M. It took approximately one year to build the homes, and no one was allowed to move in until all the homes had been built. If at the end of construction, any man was found short of the required number of hours worked, he and his family were prohibited from occupying their new home until he completed the hours while working as a member of the next project. The delayed move-in did not stop the families from sightseeing. Mary Brookins, a member of one of the Flanner House home-building families, recalled walking to the building site with her three children in tow to check on the work being done by her husband and the other men. When her house was under construction, she came by more often, to make sure the guys were not "sloughing off."[43]

At the conclusion of construction, the families secured loans from a pre-arranged lender and purchased their houses for approximately $12,500. The time they had spent building was used as a down payment. Consequently, at the end of construction each man had essentially paid a 25 percent down payment, or $3,125.[44] Flanner House, in keeping with its charter as a social service agency, operated the program as a not-for-profit endeavor.

City leaders labeled the Flanner House home-building project a tremendous success. They were not alone. In community folklore, African Americans continue to cite the Flanner House homes as a successful challenge to the inadequate housing that plagued the city. During the fourteen years between 1950 and 1964, Flanner House built more than 330 homes. Of those families who owned Flanner House homes, only four suffered foreclosure. The program was the primary manner in which African Americans bought newly built homes in Indianapolis. Curiously, Flanner House's home-building program repudiated the findings of its own 1939 symposium which had concluded that low family incomes hindered African American movement into quality homes.[45] Judging from the success Flanner House had in attracting middle-income African Americans to participate in the house building, it is evident that low income levels did not retard black home purchases as much as did overt racial residential restrictions.

Furthermore, a critical assessment of the program brings claims of its success into question. The house-building program masked the fact that Flanner House helped maintain segregated housing patterns. Flanner House built homes in areas already inhabited by African Americans. None of its projects came close to stretching the geographic limitations African Americans faced in Indianapolis's segregated housing market.[46] Moreover, between 1950 and 1960, the period when Flanner House was most active in home building, home ownership for whites increased from 60.7 percent to 67.2 percent, while home ownership for non-whites went only from 44.2 percent to 44.9 percent. The Flanner House program was successful, but only in adding to the quality of homes and not in significantly adding to the overall number. Critics, not the least of whom was Henry Richardson, an old warrior in civil rights activities, accused Flanner House of creating a ghetto. Richardson pressed Cleo Blackburn to quit working with the city's power structure to the detriment of the majority of African Americans. Richardson wrote, "Flanner House Homes and its backers . . . have gone on record opposed to constitutional open occupancy

housing for Negroes. You just can't ride two horses at the same time and neither can you demand equality and beg for favors at the same time." Blackburn
replied, "We must just accept the things that we can't do anything about . . .
and then with moderation try to do something about the things that we can
help to change."[47] In the brief dialogue between the two men lay the dilemma
of protest through self-help. Richardson wanted a more comprehensive assault
on housing segregation, one that brought greater redress for the majority of
African Americans. Blackburn, who worked intricately with the Indianapolis
power structure, believed that helping some acquire quality housing was better than the existing reality where those of means were forced to live in substandard housing.

With an average of twenty-three homes built per year, Flanner House's
efforts hardly alleviated the pressing housing need.[48] Moreover, despite the ex-
emplary loan repayment history of Flanner House home builders, mortgage
lenders in Indianapolis were still reluctant to grant mortgages to African
Americans or to anyone who chose to live in an African American neighborhood. The only reason the Flanner House home-building project could continue was that there was a steady supply of clients ready to get involved with
the project. Although it made no sense for financially stable families to devote
a year to building a home when they could take out a mortgage and move in
immediately, they built Flanner homes because banks would not lend them
money to hire contractors to build for them, and real estate agents would not
show them homes in areas where they were not allowed to live. The home-building project was discontinued only after financial institutions, many of them
headquartered outside of Indianapolis, began lending money regardless of race,
and after Indianapolis finally accepted federal funds to build additional public
housing.[49] The demand for Flanner House homes then ceased almost immediately, and the program was discontinued.

The legislative initiative that had the greatest potential to add to the number of homes available to African Americans was an open housing ordinance.
In 1963, at a conference sponsored by Governor Matthew Welsh, William T.
Ray, the president of Ray Realty and an African American, told a group of 175
real estate brokers, lenders, contractors, and civil rights workers from all over
Indiana that "Negro home seekers have no freedom of choice." Of the "4,500
single family new and used residences" offered for sale recently in the Indianapolis area, only 100 were available to "Negroes." Rental opportunities were
worse. No existing large apartment complex had a black resident. After lunch,
Governor Welsh outlined the state's alternatives. He warned that if private businesses did not remove the intolerable barriers to open occupancy, then the state
would have to enact laws ensuring fair housing.[50] Belatedly, and after an extensive self-help program, Indianapolis African Americans were ready to emphasize efforts in the legislative process. While Flanner House built houses,

Willard Ransom, state president of the Indiana NAACP, pressured the Democratic Party to make open housing a component of the party platform. In an interview Ransom recalled, "We never intended to let up on housing. We never did. We were always fighting the housing battle."[51]

Prompted by prevailing conditions and the governor's strong statements, Indianapolis's Democratic mayor, John Barton, commissioned the drafting of open housing legislation.[52] Reverend James L. Cummings and Rufus Kuykendall, the only two black members on the city council, sponsored General Ordinance 56-1964, which would have made it illegal to refuse to rent, lease, sell, or finance housing solely on the grounds of race, religion, or national origin.[53] Cummings and Kuykendall were the only council members present at the press conference announcing the proposed ordinance. They were accompanied, however, by a group of religious leaders, black and white, who supported the idea of fair housing in Indianapolis. Additional support came from the mayor's human rights commission. J. Griffin Crump, director of the commission, offered his office's full support for the measure and urged the other council members to support the open housing ordinance. Crump argued that an injustice existed, and that it would only get worse with the construction of a new highway, work on which was due to begin in 1965. Of the 4,700 homes expected to be razed for the project, more than half belonged to African Americans.[54] It was in the early 1960s that political alliance with the Democrats finally bore fruit. At both the state and local level, African Americans formed a vital constituency for the Democrats.

Not all factions were excited about the existence of a law prohibiting selective, discriminatory real estate practices. It did not take long for the Indianapolis Real Estate Board to issue a statement through its president, Richard H. Graves, alleging that an open housing ordinance would be "an invasion of the basic right of property ownership and freedom of choice."[55] Graves further argued that an ordinance was not needed because many homes were now sold using Federal Housing Administration or Veterans Administration loans, both of which were available to individuals regardless of race.

Prompted by Graves' comments and the position of the Indianapolis Real Estate Board, the Congress of Racial Equality (CORE) charged the board with discrimination, and they had ample evidence of the Indianapolis Real Estate Board's nefarious actions. The board had a "white only" clause in its by-laws, the only metropolitan real estate group in the United States with such a restriction.[56] CORE specifically cited the board for the following infractions: systematic exclusion of African Americans from the board; promotion of opposition to a fair housing ordinance in the white community; refusal to show African Americans houses in white neighborhoods; and, most pointedly, lack of real concern about city housing problems.[57] Given the board's claims that the housing crisis was overrated, it was easy for many black citizens to agree that the board was insensitive, if not guilty of more selfish aims.[58]

Real estate interests believed some sort of legislation was inevitable. Governor Welsh had already spearheaded civil rights legislation through the legislature, and his threat to enact open housing legislation was well heeded. By the time the council met to decide the ordinance's fate, it was apparent that much had happened behind the scenes. Max Brydenthal, Democratic council member, offered four amendments for the council's consideration. Two of them, the removal of a 30-day jail term if agents refused to pay a fine and an exemption of multiple dwellings or apartments if the owner inhabited one of the units, were relatively minor. But the other two amendments were more significant and threatened to make the ordinance almost meaningless. Brydenthal urged the council to remove the clause that prohibited real estate brokers from influencing sales by discussing with clients the possible market reaction as minorities moved to their neighborhood. And, in a direct concession to the Indianapolis Real Estate Board, Brydenthal proposed that individual owners be excluded from the ordinance. Brydenthal said his intent was to ensure that a homeowner "could sell his own house and reserve the right to discriminate, or to sell it through a broker." Cummings voted in favor of the ordinance with the amendments included. Kuykendall did not. Neither man seems to have understood the full implications of the "broker" amendment. Brokers did not sell houses; they merely found buyers for homeowners. Real estate agents could continue doing what they had been doing for years under the title of broker rather than agent.[59] J. Griffin Crump, director of the mayor's human rights commission, was right: the ordinance had as "much punch as tea at cocktail time."[60] Indianapolis residents would have to continue to struggle for fair, open housing without legislative assistance.

Brydenthal's amendments highlighted the inadequate relationship that existed between African Americans and the Democratic Party and the city's at-large political structure. African Americans had counted on the support of Democratic members of the council to uphold the spirit of the open housing legislation. Democratic politicians could assert that they had passed an ordinance while also maintaining that they had not drastically altered the city's social structure. African Americans had engaged in political negotiations, and they got something, but not much. What was evident was that significant population numbers could not be equated with political strength. It was a lesson that should have been learned earlier, given the previous inability to translate their numbers into power; nevertheless, it was a lesson they would be forced to revisit. Since negotiations with government officials had proven disappointing, it was left to citizens to enact change within their own spheres of influence.

One neighborhood that peacefully tried to change its existing racial makeup was the area around Butler University. Butler-Tarkington, as it was called, was directly in the path of African American migration. With its southern boundary at 38th Avenue, Butler-Tarkington residents began to witness demographic changes in the years after World War II. White residents in other neighborhoods faced with the same demographic shift simply moved to the suburbs. Butler-Tarkington was primarily composed of middle-class professionals and white people connected to Butler University. Instead of creating barricades to ward off integration, a progressive neighborhood association thought that the best way to protect property values was to resist white flight and work with realtors to sell homes to African Americans who shared their middle-class values.

Started in 1956 by four families, two black and two white, the Butler-Tarkington Neighborhood Association (BTNA) strove to "achieve an ideal racially integrated, beautiful neighborhood in that part of Indianapolis north of 38th Street, west of Meridian Street, south of 56th Street, and east of Route 421 and the Water Company Canal, whichever is the farthest east."[61] Their first meeting, which was called to discuss integration within the neighborhood, was sparsely attended. The second meeting, called to defend Tarkington Park from business interests, introduced BTNA as a force to be reckoned with. Neighborhood businesses eyed the run-down and neglected park as an ideal location for a parking lot. But residents urged the Metropolitan Planning Department and the city Parks Department to protect the park from destruction and to provide adequate funding to ensure a safe, sanitary play environment. BTNA was successful in getting the Parks Department to allocate sufficient funds and staff personnel to Tarkington Park. From those humble beginnings around a non-racial issue, the neighborhood association grew to be one of the most formidable neighborhood associations in Indianapolis. In some respects, their first success was indicative of the success the association would have in non-racial, structural, issues.[62]

BTNA proved that property values could be maintained in biracial neighborhoods. Furthermore, with BTNA acting as an active proponent of integration, the neighborhood did not suffer from homeowner instability. Since 1956, the Butler-Tarkington neighborhood has displayed as high an occupancy rate as any neighborhood in Indianapolis. But Butler-Tarkington's stability was not achieved by accident. Already by 1958, BTNA had addressed the problem of "panic selling," in which homeowners would quickly sell their property at the first incursion of African Americans to their neighborhood in order to receive "fair" market value. One of the early proposals to prevent panic selling included the creation of block groups to encourage residents to remain calm in the face of "natural Negro residential expansion."[63] However, BTNA intervention was not always successful. In 1961, vandals defaced two homes owned by black families living in an otherwise all-white block. The BTNA assisted the victimized families and worked to relieve tensions. Shortly after the incident, three homes in the same block were sold to white families, suggesting that the association's quick action had maintained Butler-Tarkington's reputation as a safe, desirable neighborhood.[64]

The percentage of African American residents in Butler-Tarkington grew from 8 percent in 1950 to 55 percent by 1980. If integration can be measured by the racial composition within a neighborhood's borders, then Butler-Tarkington successfully integrated its neighborhood with few negative consequences. However, one should not be confused by the term "neighborhood." Spatial segregation within Butler-Tarkington was extensive. For all of BTNA's success, one still hesitates to say true integration took place in the Butler-Tarkington neighborhood or within the BTNA. African Americans were initially hesitant to join the organization, perhaps out of recognition of the role earlier associations had played in limiting African American movement into other Indianapolis neighborhoods. Even after there was some demonstration of goodwill, African Americans did not eagerly join in the BTNA's events. Furthermore, African Americans were effectively sequestered in the southern portion of the neighborhood, near 38th Street, where blocks were primarily African American–occupied, while blocks nearer 56th Street, the northern boundary of Butler-Tarkington, remained almost exclusively white-owned.[65]

The BTNA apparently felt the informal goal of neighborhood stability was equal in importance to its constitutional goal of an "ideal racially integrated, beautiful neighborhood." In 1956, BTNA members were concerned with panic selling by white residents as African Americans approached the neighborhood's southern borders. By 1969, the BTNA changed its emphasis and was concerned with importing enough white residents to maintain integration. An internal housing association policy read:

> The BTNA area has been faced over the last 15 years with a gradual increase of all-Negro blocks, one by one, from south to north across the neighborhood. About 60% of the households in the total area are Negro. The blocks south of 46th Street are with few exceptions all Negro. In the entire neighborhood, no blocks remain all white. The basic problem at this time is to make the rate of white move-ins greater than the rate of Negro move-ins.[66]

The BTNA sought and received a $60,000 grant from Neighborhood Housing Opportunities (NHO), a non-profit corporation organized to promote integrated housing throughout Marion County. BTNA members discussed supplementing the NHO money with a grant from the Ford Foundation for the express purpose of alleviating some of the moving costs for white families. The BTNA bought advertising space in two national magazines, *Saturday Review* and the *New Republic,* in an effort to attract prospective white buyers. Black families were "welcomed warmly," but told of the racial imbalance and were encouraged and assisted to seek homes in "predominantly white blocks within

Figures 3.1 to 3.4. As the series of maps depicts, racial integration of the Butler-Tarkington neighborhood began at the southern border in 1940. African Americans moved steadily northward during the ensuing decades.

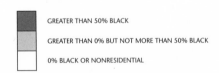

GREATER THAN 50% BLACK

GREATER THAN 0% BUT NOT MORE THAN 50% BLACK

0% BLACK OR NONRESIDENTIAL

Figure 3.1. Butler-Tarkington neighborhood, 1940.
Source: Census Block Statistics.
Map created by Dr. Timothy Kenny.

GREATER THAN 50% BLACK

GREATER THAN 0% BUT NOT MORE THAN 50% BLACK

0% BLACK OR NONRESIDENTIAL

Figure 3.2. Butler-Tarkington neighborhood, 1950.
Source: Census Block Statistics.
Map created by Dr. Timothy Kenny.

but especially outside of BTNA's boundaries."[67] Indianapolis's best example of
a middle-class, integrated neighborhood was plagued with the same priorities
found in other neighborhoods, namely, that landowners cherished property values more than fair, open housing.

By 1960, the rate of home ownership in Indianapolis was higher than in most

GREATER THAN 50% BLACK

GREATER THAN 0% BUT NOT MORE THAN 50% BLACK

0% BLACK OR NONRESIDENTIAL

Figure 3.3. Butler-Tarkington neighborhood, 1960.
Source: Census Block Statistics.
Map created by Dr. Timothy Kenny.

northern cities for both African Americans and whites. And even though most African American homes were older and located in the center city, census records show that nearly half of all black families owned their homes. The percentage would swell if the census recognized homes purchased on contract, a technique often thought of not as debt repayment but as paying rent. But census

GREATER THAN 50% BLACK

GREATER THAN 0% BUT NOT MORE THAN 50% BLACK

0% BLACK OR NONRESIDENTIAL

Figure 3.4. Butler-Tarkington neighborhood, 1970.
Source: Census Block Statistics.
Map created by Dr. Timothy Kenny.

numbers only tell part of the story. The houses around Indiana Avenue had fallen into tremendous disrepair, no doubt because of lenders' long-standing unwillingness to make home renovation loans in the area. As had been the case in other "blighted" areas, city leaders believed it easier, and more politically expedient, to clear the neighborhood rather than expend the effort to revitalize a neighborhood, which had once been the trademark of the African American community.

In a very real way, the death knell of the physical community surrounding Indiana Avenue came with the construction of I-465, I-65, and Indiana University–Purdue University Indianapolis (IUPUI). To facilitate easy access from the burgeoning suburbs (which were populated mainly by whites) to the downtown business district, Indianapolis city officials badgered Indiana legislators for funds to construct a highway. They did not have to pester the legislature very long before permission was granted and funds allocated.[68] Construction began in 1960 and was complete by the mid-1970s. The Indianapolis interstate highway system is typical of the hub-spoke-rim pattern of many urban freeway systems. The beltway, I-465, is a fifty-seven-mile loop. It was completed in 1970, following a decade of construction. An inner loop encloses the downtown area on three sides and serves as the hub for the spokes of I-70 and I-65. Three other interstate highways intersect the beltway, and six United States highways radiate from the city.[69]

In addition to providing access from the suburbs to downtown, highway construction also removed slums. Highway and university construction was a viable way of ridding the city of some of its worst eyesores while simultaneously serving suburban communities. John Walls, senior deputy mayor from 1968 to 1973 and executive director of the Greater Indianapolis Progress Committee, noted the collateral benefits of construction on the city's west side. "Among other things, it had the very good side effect of cleaning a slum, and I'm sure that was a big part of the thoughts in his [Frank McKinney, senior chairman of Greater Indianapolis Progress Committee and board trustee of Indiana University] mind during the planning."[70] City and state officials planned to remove families in the highway's path, well aware that the existing housing market could not absorb the displaced families.[71] Highway I-65 destroyed the neighborhoods that supported the remaining commercial ventures on Indiana Avenue and helped force the dispersal of the largest black population in Indianapolis.

The same scenario existed when plans were made to build the IUPUI campus. Built in 1967, the university was to occupy the area between Military Park and Indiana Avenue. By the time of construction, much of the area, including Lockefield Gardens, had fallen into disrepair. University official Dr. Joseph Taylor recalled, "There were just shacks there. Just shacks. Many of the homes were boarded up or should have been. Placing the university here was an improvement."[72] Ida Edelin, social worker and project personnel director for the Flanner House home project, recalled the two-story outhouse investigators found while appraising one home's value in the late 1960s.[73]

Some independent observers believed that the dispersal of 7,500 to 15,000 African Americans presented Indianapolis with its best opportunity to achieve residential integration. In preparation for a series devoted to race relations in

Figure 3.5. Two-story outhouse on IUPUI campus grounds, 1961.
Source: IUPUI University Library Special Collections and Archives.

Indianapolis, Harrison J. Ullmann, a reporter for the *Indianapolis Star,* investigated the city's "reaction to civil rights and integration." Ullmann concluded that many of the prerequisites for open housing were in place. Most notably, Ullmann highlighted the income level of middle-class African Americans able to afford housing, an open housing ordinance, new federal regulations that eliminated discriminatory practices in FHA and VA mortgage lending, and, most importantly, a recent change in the attitudes of white, middle-class residents, who no longer fought integration. Ullmann was cautiously optimistic, but Deputy Mayor John Walls probably best characterized the attitudes of those in the path of the new highway and university:

> Housing was in fairly short supply and as a matter of fact the suggestion of the expansion of the university on the Westside created some concern on the part of the black community, because most of the folks living in that area were minorities and that, plus the creation of the interstate highway system created, I suppose, a major part of the concern that the black community had regarding housing in the community. They—here as elsewhere—were fearful that renewal meant displacement, which, of course, it did.[74]

IUPUI's placement was particularly vexing. City officials understandably believed that the campus would be the cornerstone of redevelopment for the area.[75] No doubt their vision has proven correct as the area, including the remaining buildings at Lockefield Gardens, is currently part of downtown gentrification. However, the cost was significant, as the campus helped displace the very people an urban campus was intended to serve.[76] No one could easily dispute that the area surrounding IUPUI and Indiana Avenue was in tremendous disrepair. It is equally indisputable that too often the price of urban renewal, especially in black neighborhoods, was the clearing of land and the dislocation of residents. Neighborhood residents were faced with two equally unpleasant options. They could sell their homes for a price that was grossly inadequate for purchasing a home elsewhere in Indianapolis, or they could fight eminent domain.

African Americans did not sit idly by while their neighborhoods were razed. John Torian, a young, black community activist, began Homes Before Highways, an organization dedicated to the fair relocation of residents forced to move by highway construction. Few records remain of the organization, but John Liell, a sociologist at IUPUI, recalled that Torian's group was instrumental in helping residents get fair compensation for their homes. Charles Hardy, a real estate officer for IUPUI, disputed Liell's assessment of the organization:

> I think it goes a bit far to call it [Homes Before Highways] an organization. It was a group of people, an assemblage of people, if you will. And, you know, call a meeting and—it was never a meeting. It was always gonna [sic] be a mass rally, you know. You never had meetings—in a church basement someplace or church or any place you could find a hall, and [you] hope to fill the hall, and make a lot of noise, and generate publicity for your cause. And the highway department was the big target. . . . Did they try—did the people who were the activist organizers, would-be organizers—did they try to appeal in both the black community and the white community? The answer's yes. It was somewhat successful, but it did not last very long or have significant impact.[77]

Despite Hardy's assessment, area residents remembered Torian as a strong advocate of homeowner rights. Homes Before Highways battled city and state officials, urging them to pay the prevailing price for the cost of a new home rather than the market price. The market value of homes in the Indiana Avenue area was dramatically lower than in other areas of the city, which affected the ability of homeowners near the "Avenoo" from purchasing homes elsewhere. Torian was successful in getting public agencies to pay more for the homes, but only after a good number of people had already accepted a lower amount.[78]

By the 1960s, slum clearance had been an issue for nearly thirty years. In the 1930s, the Indianapolis city council had forestalled clearance efforts by refusing to create a local housing authority. Council members feared that a housing authority would provide public housing in direct competition to privately funded initiatives. While Gary, Fort Wayne, Kokomo, and many other cities in Indiana undertook slum clearance projects during the Great Depression, Indianapolis allowed people to live in shacks less than a mile from downtown.[79] Even when city inspectors condemned properties as unfit for human habitation, they were reluctant to evict inhabitants because they knew that no other options existed. One study found that of 666 houses found unsuitable for habitation, only 130 were demolished.[80]

In 1968, radio station WFBM commissioned Frank N. Magid Associates, a research organization based in Iowa, to study the city's black community. When they asked respondents what three major problems faced black residents of Indianapolis, almost every respondent included inadequate housing.[81] In 1969, another study commissioned by the Metropolitan Planning Department of Marion County and conducted by Hammer, Greene, Silver & Associates (Hammer) succinctly detailed Indianapolis's housing problem. The Hammer study demonstrated that a fully efficient housing market would add new units each year sufficient to meet the existing need. Further, an efficient system, in theory, would rid itself of substandard housing as standard units became available.[82] The problem, as Hammer correctly deduced, was that the process in Indianapolis was stalled through "actual or potential" racial discrimination. According to Hammer's research, some 5,000 black families desired and could afford but were not able to get higher quality or better-located housing of their choice.[83] Higher-income African Americans were unable to move into areas befitting their income level, which then forced lower-income African Americans to continue their occupancy of substandard units. To the theorists writing for Hammer, the solution was simple: governmental agencies in Indianapolis needed to enforce existing housing codes, demolish substandard housing, and eliminate barriers to free access for the existing housing stock. If city officials acted appropriately and consistently, the Indianapolis housing market would normalize and operate efficiently.[84] In essence, by linking the African American housing situation to city growth, Hammer said that if the city fixed the African American housing problem, they would simultaneously fix Indianapolis's housing problem.

The two studies, both done in the late 1960s, echoed the results found by Flanner House in 1937. Indeed, little had changed in the ensuing thirty years. Housing options for African Americans in Indianapolis were consistently limited. Since the years before World War II, there simply were not enough dwellings to house the population adequately. In the 1950s, Indianapolis leaders, concerned with the city's reputation as a dirty and backward city, began to renovate the most blighted areas. However, it was not the city of Indianapolis that undertook the renovation as much as it was African Americans, who tried to build homes once obstructions were removed. These efforts provided substantially better housing, but did not add to the overall number of available houses; they merely got rid of the most odious examples. Throughout the period under study, one factor remained constant: Whites effectively blocked African Americans from living in more desirable areas despite intense efforts undertaken by African Americans to combat the prevailing conditions. By the late 1960s, Indianapolis leaders realized that its housing wounds were self-inflicted, and it began to accept federal funding, enforce building codes, and urge financial institutions to ease redlining practices. But in many ways, the issue was moot. Whites no longer needed racial covenants and neighborhood associations to block African American movement into white neighborhoods. The economic gap between whites and African Americans had grown sufficiently that economic realities provided the most effective barrier. African Americans' polite, systemic protest had produced victory when it no longer mattered.

4

"You're Tired, Chile"

Work Opportunities and Restrictions
for Indianapolis's African Americans

In 1934, the federal government's Public Works Administration commissioned the distinguished Indianapolis painter John Wesley Hardrick to paint a mural. This mural, entitled *Workers,* depicts three African American laborers pouring molten ore into molds, their faces aglow from the heat and light emanating from smelting furnaces. Behind the central characters are other black men toiling near other furnaces. Hardrick knew his subject well. While a student at the John Herron School of Art, Hardrick worked at National Malleable, an Indianapolis company that produced steel containers. Hardrick presented his painting to Russell Lane, principal of Crispus Attucks High School, for placement in the school's foyer. Lane accepted the gift but refused to install the mural at Attucks. He thought the depiction of African American men employed in such unsavory labor would dampen student aspirations. Surely, Lane reasoned, Attucks students could aspire to more than unskilled manual labor, despite the respect Hardrick accorded the laborers.[1]

Lane's position highlighted the troubling reality African Americans encountered. Although the local labor market rarely allowed African Americans into managerial and technical positions, African American community leaders nevertheless fought to expand opportunities. They trained young African Americans for positions not yet open to them, and they petitioned local employers, formally and informally, to expand employment opportunities. They attempted to display African American preparedness and civility to show that they deserved wider employment opportunities.[2]

The attempt to broaden African American labor opportunities was almost exclusively a local matter. The National Urban League, which had gained respect throughout the United States for aiding African American workers, failed to initiate a chapter in Indianapolis until 1965, and no other national organization filled the void. Left to combat the labor inequities without meaningful assistance from national organizations, Indianapolis's African Americans employed methods to attack job segregation and unemployment similar to those they had used against educational and housing segregation: they presented evidence of the problem to city and business leaders, and they worked, largely in biracial forums, to reverse the tide of discrimination. As was the case in previous instances, their course of action was inherently tedious and frustrating, and its successes were few and far between. Eventual relief, albeit limited, came only when African Americans, working largely with the Democratic Party, helped enact statewide reform in the form of fair employment legislation and a civil rights act. But although such victories were momentous, they were essentially hollow victories that proved ineffectual in substantially raising African American economic prospects.

Central to the debate between Hardrick and Lane were the issues of limited job opportunities and economic aspirations for African Americans. While striving for desirable jobs, African Americans, in large measure, were relegated to menial positions. Notwithstanding many initiatives to alter that reality, the condition held through the 1960s. Perhaps the respondent to a survey conducted in 1938 by Flanner House, a local social service agency, was prophetic when talking of her children's future: "Well, they'll just be laborers, that's about all. They are too young yet, and I've just about given up. It has been so hard."[3] In a sense, discussing labor opportunities for African Americans is like deconstructing a one-note song, but the song played to a familiar tune, one well known to city inhabitants. African Americans pressed for change and increased opportunity, and white business, labor, and political leaders forestalled their advancement through legal and extralegal means. African American worked within the system to effect change, perhaps out of fear that they would lose what they had already achieved. For while African Americans were not employed in the most desirable jobs, they did enjoy a favorable employment rate when compared to African Americans in nearby cities.

Despite Lane's fears that Hardrick's depiction would bridle student ambition, manual labor was a reality probably well known to most Attucks students. Indeed, in the early decades of the twentieth century, laborers in iron and steel constituted one of the three positions categorized by the United States Commerce Department in which blacks outnumbered whites in the Indianapolis labor market, even though whites vastly outnumbered blacks in the workforce as a whole.[4] During the 1930s most blacks and many whites were happy to have a job in an industrial setting—or any setting for that matter. That blacks were working in the hottest and dirtiest part of the industrial plant was not unusual.[5] In northern communities throughout the United States, blacks frequently occupied the lowest rungs of the industrial ladder. The debate that Hardwick and Lane pursued was one that African Americans had faced for some time: how

Table 4.1. Percent of Civilian Labor Force 14 and Over Unemployed

When compared to regional neighbors, African American men and women enjoyed the lowest unemployment rate, a condition that was common for most of the period.

SMSA	Males W*	Males NW	Females W	Females NW
Chicago	3.6	11.0	3.1	12.6
Cincinnati	4.2	15.5	3.1	10.3
Columbus	4.3	9.6	3.4	9.9
Indianapolis	2.7	9.3	2.3	9.1

*Race is denoted as appears in census: NW, when non-whites are the reference group.

Source: 1950 Census, Population Statistics.

to increase economic opportunity without endangering accrued benefits, however minimal.

Indianapolis laborers, both black and white, were intricately tied to increased manufacturing development during the early decades of the twentieth century. Indianapolis's promoters had not yet surrendered hope that their city would overcome Cincinnati's early lead to become the principal economic center in the region. Their plan was to make Indianapolis a "hub" of railroad transportation. In their vision of the future, railroad lines would bring freight to the city from all over the country, where it would be unloaded and rerouted to other areas.

Indianapolis fulfilled its goal of becoming a hub, but highways, rather than railways, brought produce and manufactured goods to the city. By 1920, Indianapolis had become a major automobile manufacturer, producing cars such as the Stutz Bearcat and the Duesenberg. Some firms were ephemeral, while others, aided by their proximity to the Indianapolis Motor Speedway, helped establish the city as a major player in automobile production. The presence of automobile manufacturers and other industries did much to diversify the local economy and expand job opportunities.[6]

Some African Americans found work in the developing industries, but full employment was still a problem for the community. A report filed by Flanner House documented the state of African American life in Indianapolis in 1939. It included comments from a woman who said, "Well, son, getting a job is the greatest difficulty for us colored folks." The interviewer tried to explain the relationship between education and jobs, the reality of a marketplace economy, and the effects of the national depression. The woman responded, "I don't know any of those high falutin' reasons, but I know we need jobs."[7]

The middle-class professionals who had been so instrumental in leading the fight against housing restrictions and school segregation largely led the fight for increased job opportunities, utilizing the time-worn practices of negotiation, compromise, and subtle pressure. Employment was one area where middle-class and working-class interests seemingly diverged. African American professionals could advise moderation and patience because their African American clients and patients were able to pay their fees even while working menial jobs. Their attention was more squarely focused on school and housing desegregation than on employment reform because the former had a more direct effect on their lives. Consequently, while middle-class leaders led the fight, their status conditioned their method and strategy. They advised African Americans to clean up their act and become paragons of virtue as a form of protest. Starling James, president of the Federation of Associated Clubs (FAC), an association dedicated to the promotion of social, civic, and economic benefits for the African American community, wrote a series of articles for the *Indianapolis Recorder*. Entitled "Guide Right," these articles advised African Americans to "be well scrubbed behind the ears" and cautioned that "manners are one of the prerequisites of an outstanding personality."[8] James represented the most consistently political organization in Indianapolis, yet his counsel was consistent with middle-class precepts and values. Leaders mistakenly believed that African American emphases on deportment and character would translate into greater job opportunities. Flanner House, which had an interracial board of directors, focused its efforts on self-help initiatives, including job training, an approach that was appealing both to African American and white civic leaders.

Flanner House was the most widely recognized social service agency in Indianapolis. The management of Flanner House was never solely African American. The board of directors was consistently largely composed of white community leaders who solicited funds and oversaw operations of the Flanner House Guild. The guild aimed to help people who were willing to help themselves. Its earliest programs included instruction in millinery, sewing, first aid, and cooking. In 1908, the guild created the Flanner House Guild Rescue Home, where job training and education classes were to aid women's search for suitable employment. In 1935, Cleo Blackburn, a black social worker, assumed the superintendent position at Flanner House, and under his direction, Flanner House worked to provide social services to the black community. Flanner House was instrumental in providing health care and health education for community residents. To this day, it continues to act as a community health outlet, providing visiting nurse services and annual inoculations.

After a visit in 1941, Millie M. Peck, a prominent New York social worker and executive secretary of the National Federation of Settlements, favorably reviewed Flanner House. Despite finding the building and facilities deplorable and "inadequate," Peck praised the child and adult training classes. Fay Williams, an African American attorney and community organizer, moved to Indianapolis from Washington, D.C., in 1943 and almost immediately recognized Flanner House's contradictory role in the community. "Flanner House was seen as a great service. Its childcare program and its education program, sewing classes, canning, the Morgan health center was over there. In terms of services, it was indisputable. But in terms of empowerment issues there was a real separation." Williams did not consider training classes a means of empowerment. Officials at Flanner House believed that efforts like these provided African American residents with the wherewithal to be self-reliant and thrifty. Reflecting the philosophy of its director, Cleo Blackburn, Flanner House left the more visible empowerment practices to other groups.[9]

Flanner House and its administrators provided important social welfare leadership, but they chose not to extend their leadership to other areas. Perhaps Williams was right: they could not step outside their traditional boundaries and still receive financial support. In the eyes of local business and philanthropic leaders, Flanner House had become so pivotal that they saw it as the only institution needed to address the black community's problems. It received funds from private donations as well as from Community Chest, a local organization akin to the United Way. Indianapolis administrators often applauded and supported Flanner House's efforts while simultaneously distancing themselves from the efforts of more controversial groups that proposed legislation to address long-standing racial issues. It is easy to understand why Flanner House appealed to politicians and bureaucrats. One of its founding doctrines was self-help. Supporting Flanner House initiatives often meant aiding citizens who had already pledged efforts of their own, a much more politically sensitive practice than simply granting aid for politicians who were wary of perceptions that they assisted those who could help themselves. Far too often, the city supported Flanner House to the exclusion of any other organization. A wholly Indianapolis entity, it did not reek of outside control or hidden agendas. Whites often accepted Flanner House as the sole voice for black concerns, and, consequently, issues that it did not champion were seen as insignificant, outside the purview of organizational aid, or, worst of all, tainted in some respect. As a result, Flanner House made all other organizational efforts seem illegitimate and trivial in the eyes of city administrators, politicians, and benefactors.

Blackburn was deserving of the praise he received for directing Flanner House's development, but he was also responsible for much of the criticism the agency received for remaining removed from political affairs. Perhaps because financial support for Flanner House primarily came from white benefactors, Blackburn made a conscious effort to avoid any issue that was overtly political. Blackburn's suspicions were not altogether fanciful. Many local business leaders were leery of organizations that were not locally controlled. They feared that an "outside" organization would press too hard to change the existing labor situation in Indianapolis.

The existence of Flanner House may help to explain why a local chapter of the Urban League was not formed until 1965.[10] Many supporters of Flanner House believed that an Urban League chapter would only duplicate the job procurement and training programs already in place. Fay Williams saw it differently. "Cleo [Blackburn], in my belief, had to make his peace with those ultra-conservatives to get his agenda through; had to separate himself from organizations like the NAACP. Cleo and Flanner House supporters felt that the Urban League wasn't needed here. They didn't want it. They also felt the United Way wasn't going to support black agencies."[11] Those who opposed the establishment of an Urban League chapter pointed to Flanner House and the Association for Merit Employment (AME), a private, non-profit organization founded by the Quakers' American Friends Service Committee in 1952, as examples of voluntary, cooperative initiatives to increase African American employment.[12] The AME's efforts were well-intentioned, but their strategy of inducing local companies to hire African Americans through voluntary means was ultimately unsuccessful. At best, the AME showed that African American labor constraints were widespread and systemic. At worse, they delayed the deployment of more aggressive protest strategies, and, in particular, the founding of a local Urban League chapter.

The AME was the first organization in Indianapolis to focus solely on increasing job opportunities for African Americans. Composed of local retail and industrial executives, the AME dedicated itself to working with management, labor, and other affected groups and agencies in implementing the policy and practice of employing and upgrading the "best qualified applicant for each vacancy regardless of the applicant's race, religion or national origin." Flanner House was also concerned with job training and education, but the directors often were distracted by other pressing concerns. However, Flanner House worked in concert with the AME, often training workers that the AME eventually tried to place in retail and industrial occupations. Operating on a purely cooperative basis, the AME responded to job discrimination and unemployment by attempting to convince Indianapolis business owners that fair employment was in the city's best interest. The AME invited companies to place personnel directors or other executives involved in hiring and promotion on the committee and have them lead the effort to find employment in their companies for black workers. It was able to attract some of the largest, best-known employers in the city. L. S. Ayres and William Block's (both local retail department stores), RCA, Lilly Pharmaceuticals, and Allison (manufacturers of engines and transmissions) were represented on the committee. The committee also collected and disseminated information pertaining to jobs open to all races, counseled training agencies on employment opportunities for members of minority groups, and encouraged local businesses to develop and use the special skills and talents of minority members.

The AME became so entrenched and central to Indianapolis's labor efforts that it eventually became part of the United Fund of Indianapolis, the primary charity vehicle in the city. Indeed, William L. Schloss, vice president of admissions for the United Fund of Greater Indianapolis, denied funding for a proposed National Urban League chapter on the grounds that Flanner House and the AME adequately served the African American community. But although white city officials cited the AME's efforts as satisfactory, the AME records indicate otherwise. In 1963, the AME could only find jobs for 76 of the African Americans who applied to it for assistance.[13] In 1964, even more job hunters filed applications, but, in this its last year of operation, the AME could place only 64 of the 636 applicants. Despite the visible presence of the AME, the organization was ill equipped for the task. Merely making employers aware of the supply of trained potential employees did not ease unemployment for African American workers. Even the AME found their own record unsatisfactory, and, in 1965, they led the fight to bring the Urban League to Indianapolis.[14]

The absence of a National Urban League chapter hampered the advancement of Indianapolis's black workers. One of the most important functions of the National Urban League was the tracking and documenting of black workers and their condition. The Urban League had long attempted to establish a presence in Indianapolis, and in 1916, the organization sent a representative to the city with instructions to establish a branch chapter. The representative, Eugene Kunckle Jones, executive secretary of the National Urban League, considered Indianapolis a "complex problem." Jones recognized the existence of social service agencies and met with representatives of Associated Charities and the superintendent of the Flanner Guild settlement house. After Jones left Indianapolis, officials from the various charity organizations decided to delay creating a National Urban League chapter in Indianapolis. They deemed existing services sufficient to the demand. Many whites believed that an "outside" organization could not do a better job than local groups. Supporters of the Urban League, including the FAC, the NAACP, and several ministers, highlighted Urban League successes in other cities and argued that a more coordinated effort in Indianapolis would bring similar results. In 1965, Indianapolis finally established an Urban League chapter, decades after Chicago (1917), Detroit (1916), Pittsburgh (1918), and nearby Gary, Indiana (1946).[15] Nationally, the Urban League strove to achieve peaceful, cooperative relationships with industrial and commercial leaders. In keeping with that goal, they did not establish a chapter in Indianapolis until both black and white citizens invited them to come to town.[16] The policy of not forming a local chapter until invited, first established in 1916 and reaffirmed many times thereafter, hindered the collection of reliable local labor statistics and retarded the movement of African Americans into wider labor arenas. Without valid statistics and an organization pressing for reform, employers alleged that black employment was improving, while black leaders continued to preach patience to African American laborers who knew that no dramatic change was underway.

Throughout much of the twentieth century, African American males were represented in most of the job categories identified by the United States census; however, just as Hardrick had depicted, they were most visibly represented as laborers and helpers in the iron and steel industries and the building construction trade.[17] Blacks were well-represented at most of the meat packing plants, but, as in Chicago and Milwaukee, they held the most dangerous and lowest-paying jobs.[18] Despite the emerging manufacturing economy, a good percentage of blacks occupied jobs that had little or nothing to do with expanding industrialism. Thirty-five percent of the black male workforce worked in domestic and personal service. Of those, more than half worked as janitors, sextons, porters, or servants. African American women dominated the domestic and personal service positions. More than 90 percent of black women in Indianapolis working outside of the home were employed as domestic servants, and African American women made up almost 80 percent of the total domestic servant workforce.[19]

In his study of Cleveland, Kenneth Kusmer argued that in cities with high concentrations of immigrants, employers hired fewer African Americans for skilled jobs. He further argued that the relatively high percentage of blacks engaged in skilled trades in Indianapolis in the 1890s and shortly thereafter can be partly explained by the relatively small immigrant population, a condition more common in southern cities than among northern cities of comparable size. If Kusmer is correct, one would expect less "occupational ghettoization" in cities with a small foreign-born population. But in Indianapolis, which had a small foreign-born population, African Americans did experience noticeable occupational ghettoization. The 1930 census shows remarkable similarity between Indianapolis and more ethnically diverse cities. Using Kusmer's Cleveland as a standard, one finds that 13 percent of the men employed in the transportation and communications industries were black, compared to 15 percent in Indianapolis. Cincinnati and Columbus, Ohio, reported 16 and 20 percent respectively. In each city, blacks were most likely to be chauffeurs or truck or tractor drivers.[20] Although African Americans were gainfully employed, they were found only in specific areas performing tasks categorized by race. The 1940 census indicates that more than 80 percent of Indianapolis's black labor force was employed in either private sector jobs or public emergency work.

Unemployment rates for African Americans were higher in Milwaukee and Cleveland than they were in Cincinnati and Indianapolis. In Indianapolis, the employment rate for African American men and women in 1940 was more than 90 percent; by 1960, the percentage of African American males employed had increased to 93 percent, while the rate for African American females continued to hover near the 90 percent mark.[21] Equally important, however, was the degree to which African American women were found in the workforce. In 1950, only 40 percent of black women over the age of fourteen were in the workforce; by 1960, that percentage had increased to 46 percent. Such low percentages, especially in the face of acute labor shortages in Indianapolis, indicate both the frustration in finding employment outside the arena of personal service and the limited degree to which women actively sought employment.[22]

In his demographic study of turn-of-the-century Indianapolis, Robert Barrows argued that an occupational ghetto existed for African Americans who did find work in the emerging industries, and that African Americans were heavily concentrated in the lowest occupational stratum. In the years before World War I, approximately 60 percent of the city's black male heads of household performed unskilled tasks, compared to 11 percent of whites.[23] Although those percentages were depressing, they were hardly unusual. In Milwaukee, which had a significantly smaller black population, black men and women were almost totally confined to positions of common laborer, domestic worker, or personal service worker in the pre–World War I era. That situation did not change dramatically during the interwar period.[24] In Indianapolis, the African American presence in manufacturing jobs increased from 19.2 percent in 1910 to 71 percent in 1920 and 79.6 percent as the Depression took hold. More than 60 percent of African American women worked in personal service on the eve of the Depression.[25]

Of the men in Indianapolis employed in domestic and personal service occupations, 43 percent were black as compared to 27 percent in Cleveland. There, foreign-born whites held 37 percent of the domestic and personal service occupations, while in Indianapolis only 5 percent were so employed. During the same period in each of the cities, African Americans occupied between 4 and 6 percent of professional service occupations such as lawyers and accountants. The types of jobs African Americans held did not vary much from city to city in the Midwest. Nor did the presence of foreign immigrants significantly alter the types of jobs that blacks held. While Cleveland had a significantly higher percentage of immigrants, blacks there were employed in similar occupations as those in Indianapolis.[26]

More importantly, the percentage of blacks involved in skilled trades declined with each succeeding decade. If the presence of foreign immigrants influenced African American job placement, then blacks should have occupied more skilled positions as the number of foreign immigrants declined and new skilled industrial positions emerged. But the converse was true in Indianapolis, indicating that other factors, such as union intransigence or corporate reluctance to hire African Americans, were at play.

Using an index of dissimilarity, one can trace levels of segregation in the city's industry. The index is a measure of the distribution of two groups and ranges in value from 0 to 100. If, for example, blacks made up 10 percent of the pop-

Table 4.2. Occupation by Race and Sex, Indianapolis 1950

*Data indicates that African American men and women were
most commonly employed as laborers, private household workers, or service workers.*

	Males W	Males NW	Females W	Females NW
1. Professional technical, and kindred workers	10.1	2.4	11.6	5.4
2. Managers, officials, proprietors	12.9	2.8	4.4	1.3
3. Clerical and kindred workers	9.5	4.4	37.9*	5.5
4. Sales workers	9.8	1.7	9.2	1.9
5. Craftsmen, foremen, and kindred workers	**24.1**	10.9	2.3	.9
6. Operatives and kindred workers	**21.3**	21.2	**20.2**	16.0
7. Manufacturers and kindred workers	9.1	7.8	15.2	7.1
8. Private household workers	.1	1.6	2.5	**34.4**
9. Service workers	5.1	**24.1**	9.3	**29.4**
10. Farm laborers and foremen	.5	.3	.2	.1
11. Laborers	4.7	**26.1**	.7	2.4

* Boldface numerals denote the two most common occupations.

ulation of each industry category and also made up 10 percent of the city's population, the index of dissimilarity would be zero. Correspondingly, if all members of the African American population occupied one kind of industrial position, the index value would be 100. Consequently, the higher the index values, the higher the degree of occupational segregation.[27] Based on the census's categorization of jobs in 1950, the index of dissimilarity for African American women was 44.4 percent. For black men, it was 44.7 percent. By 1960, occupational ghettoization had improved for both women and men, with women at 39.3 percent and men at 32.8 percent. In and of themselves, these numbers mean very little. They are instructive only in comparison with other settings or as a measure to chart change. The improvements represented by the index give testament to the lobbying African Americans undertook before World War II.

Beginning in 1941, after undertaking community reform efforts and ongoing efforts at self-help, blacks sought legislation to help them break through the job ceiling. In successive state legislative sessions, the NAACP, the Jewish Community Relations Council, the Federation of Associated Clubs, and a host of other groups supported a fair employment law, which would exact penalties on companies or individuals who did not comply. The Indiana Chamber of Commerce opposed the compulsory fair employment law. Employers, oppo-

Table 4.3. Occupation by Race and Sex, Indianapolis 1960

By 1960, African American men had made inroads into the formal job market as operatives while African American women maintained their significant presence as private household and service workers.

	Males W	Males NW	Females W	Females NW
1. Professional technical, and kindred workers	12.6	2.9	12.3	5.8
2. Managers, officials, proprietors	12.3	1.6	3.6	1.0
3. Clerical and kindred workers	8.4	7.7	**40.3***	16.3
4. Sales workers	8.4	1.3	9.5	1.8
5. Craftsmen, foremen, and kindred workers	**21.4**	11.4	1.4	1.0
6. Operatives and kindred workers	**13.6**	**24.4**	**14.2**	11.4
7. Manufacturers and kindred workers	6.7	9.9	5.3	2.7
8. Private household workers	.1	.6	2.6	**23.3**
9. Service workers	4.8	18.1	9.5	**25.8**
10. Farm laborers and foremen	.2	.1	.1	0
11. Laborers	4.5	**18.6**	.3	1.3

* Boldface numerals denote the two most common occupations.

nents argued, should not be penalized for choosing not to integrate their work-force. For eight years, the two opposing sides squared off in biannual legislative sessions, and on each occasion the opponents of a fair employment law won the debate. While employers often acknowledged the law's moral correctness, they found the proposed legislation impractical and unworkable. As one employer stated, "Advocates of fair employment have God and the Constitution on their side, but they don't have human nature."[28] Legislation, the employer seemed to argue, did not necessarily create a peaceful, productive workplace. Employers knew there was discriminatory hiring and job promotion, but they were more willing to continue these practices than to welcome new troubles.

Through the 1940s, organizations such as the Urban League and the NAACP intensified the fight for fair employment practices across the nation. With the onset of World War II, many of the country's manufacturers experienced labor shortages, and Indianapolis was no exception. Indeed, with Allison providing turbine engines for military aircraft and International Harvester manufacturing trucks for all branches of the armed services, industry in Indianapolis was an integral component of the country's war effort. Again mimicking other northern industrial cities, Indianapolis attracted a noticeable number of African

Table 4.4. Occupations by Race and Sex, Indianapolis 1970

It was not until 1970 that African American women
were able to find significant employment in areas other than service work.

	Males W	Males NW	Females W	Females NW
1. Professional technical, and kindred workers	14.6	6.0	**14.4***	9.5
2. Managers, officials, proprietors	11.7	2.8	3.5	1.7
3. Clerical and kindred workers	7.7	9.3	**41.0**	**26.4**
4. Sales workers	8.4	2.1	8.4	2.6
5. Craftsmen, foremen, and kindred workers	**22.8**	14.7	2.2	1.8
6. Operatives and kindred workers	**15.6**	23.8	12.7	16.2
7. Manufacturers and kindred workers	3.5	6.0	2.7	2.7
8. Private household workers	0	.2	1.5	10.6
9. Service workers	6.1	**19.0**	**14.4**	**28.5**
10. Farm laborers and foremen	.5	.2	.2	.2
11. Laborers	5.0	13.6	1.1	1.7

* Boldface numerals denote the two most common occupations.

Americans to its wartime industries. Buoyed by the increased need for African American workers, fair employment advocates throughout the state stepped up pressure on Indiana lawmakers to draft legislation prohibiting discriminatory hiring. In 1945, Indiana established the Fair Employment Practices Commission (FEPC). The FEPC did not have the authority to punish violators of fair employment practices. Foreshadowing subsequent versions of fair employment legislation, the 1945 act required only that the State Division of Labor cooperate with other state agencies and private groups in removing discrimination in employment. In other words, they made compliance with fair employment guidelines voluntary.[29]

The 1945 law provided moral exhortation, but little else. There were no provisions for reprimanding discriminatory individuals or firms. Perhaps most damning was the legislature's acceptance that unions would police themselves. The Congress of Industrial Organizations' (CIO) consistent stance for open employment made it easier to assume unions would do so too. However, not all union locals committed to a policy of minority inclusion. The FEPC did not have the authority to investigate systemic discrimination like that employed by the building trade unions. Consequently, the FEPC relied on aggrieved workers coming to them—a practice that all too rarely occurred.

Almost immediately, black representatives and organizations saw the inherent weaknesses in the FEPC legislation. The Indianapolis NAACP chapter began calling for a law "with teeth," a phrase that would be repeated often by individuals and organizations. Without providing names, the *Recorder* reported that three factories had stopped hiring blacks after World War II. Of the 3,500 workers employed at the three plants after the war, only 100 were African American, and most of them worked in maintenance positions. The *Recorder* blamed both management and the union for allowing such disparities to exist. The only remedy, editors argued, was the establishment of a Fair Employment Practices Commission with powers to penalize offending organizations.[30]

World War II did not end the widespread practice of job stratification, but lines were altered slightly. Indianapolis's blacks, like those elsewhere, took advantage of wartime labor shortages to take positions previously out of reach. But while blacks, both men and women, worked in war-production factories, they continued to face job limitations. The promotion of a black man (whose name was not reported) to lathe operator at the Curtiss-Wright plant was a newsworthy event. Within hours, however, the thirty-five other lathe operators, all white men, had walked off the job. The company and the union were at odds over an issue on which they had previously agreed. The company was bolstered in its decision to place an African American in a skilled position by Executive Order 8802, issued by Franklin D. Roosevelt in 1941, under pressure from A. Philip Randolph, president of the Brotherhood of Sleeping Car Porters. The order prohibited discrimination in war industries and the government and established the Fair Employment Practices Commission. Curtiss-Wright held the union responsible for getting the white lathe operators back on the job. The local steward, in keeping with the national CIO's efforts to foster racial diversity among its membership, could only tell the recalcitrant operators that they were in danger of losing their positions if they continued their work stoppage. Curtiss-Wright officials told the workers that they could keep their jobs, but that the black man was going to continue operating a lathe. Receiving no support from their national union and facing dismissal, the workers went back to their lathes. Shortly after the event, the white men, apparently under no coercion from union officials, threw a party for the newest operator to demonstrate their "change of heart."[31]

Perhaps the most significant addition to the African American workforce that can be directly linked to the war effort was the civil servant workers at Fort Benjamin Harrison. The civil servants were transferred to Indianapolis because Fort Benjamin Harrison was an Army payroll processing site. The workers hailed from all over the country, and many were taken aback by vestiges of Jim Crow laws in a northern city. Not beholden to Indianapolis businesses and not organized into a union, these workers soon became an effective and consistent voice for change. The NAACP, FAC, and various churches benefited from the influx of this articulate group whose jobs were guaranteed. Fay Williams, who often chided local African Americans for being afraid to fight openly for change, said of the Fort Benjamin Harrison families, "They were safe. . . . They didn't have to worry about losing their job if they spoke out against injustice. Other people in Indianapolis were afraid they'd be out of a job if they spoke out. They were really scared." Williams knew of what she spoke. She and her husband were one of the first families the federal government had transferred to Indianapolis. Andrew J. Brown, pastor at St. John's Baptist Church, identified the Fort Benjamin Harrison members as the church's most progressive members: "People who had fought for change in other cities were not going to accept second class citizenship in Indianapolis."[32]

Other black workers, like the ones employed at Curtiss-Wright, were not so secure in their jobs. Executive Order 8802 only lasted the duration of the war. Many blacks, such as Willard Ransom and Henry J. Richardson, believed that access to highly skilled jobs such as lathe operator would be closed off after the war. The final report of the wartime Fair Employment Practices Commission indicated that at the end of the war, African Americans in Indianapolis suffered a more severe setback in job opportunities than did African Americans in many other cities. Indianapolis industry rewarded seniority, with returning military men allowed to reclaim their jobs without any loss in seniority. In their traditional role as last hired, blacks were the first to be fired.[33]

Despite consistent efforts by the national office of the CIO, local labor leaders adamantly protected work opportunities for whites at the expense of black employees. A study conducted at the end of the war reported that "[b]oth the most constructive and the most restrictive forces concerning Negro employment in Indianapolis are found in labor unions."[34] Hiring and promotion in Indianapolis were found to be more restrictive than in most large cities. Of the sixty-seven large cities outside the South, Indianapolis ranked fifty-eighth in job opportunities for African Americans, meaning that only nine western and northern cities provided African Americans with fewer economic opportunities. When southern cities were included, Indianapolis ranked sixty-second, with only twenty-eight cities posting a worse record. One *Indianapolis Times* writer commented, "Indianapolis incorporates the worst aspects of the southern and northern patterns in Negro employment, either no jobs at all or only the most menial with no chance for advancement." The reporter went on to claim that Indianapolis, paradoxically, had some of the best examples of fair employment practices. She pointed to RCA-Victor, which, she argued, hired workers on the basis of individual worth and promoted them on the same basis.[35]

The journalist's assessment must have shocked Clarence Wood, a black worker at RCA-Victor. Wood had a degree in business, with a specialty in accounting, from Indiana University, but he was unable to find a job commensurate with his skills in Indianapolis and eventually took a job on the loading dock at RCA-Victor. Wood certainly found that RCA-Victor practiced occupational segregation. He recalled that most of the workers in his area were black and that throughout the plant, blacks held menial positions.[36] The *Times* reporter's contradictory observation neatly established the problem of African American employment in Indianapolis. Alberta Murphy recalled that her husband had no trouble finding work and frequently changed jobs before settling down at a metals manufacturing company. Lawrence Brookins offered a similar sentiment. The only problem he had was finding a job near his home. He eventually found work at Union Carbide in 1946 and worked there for thirty-seven years. Brookins's commute from his home in the Martindale-Brightwood neighborhood to Union Carbide in Speedway took more than an hour by bus. At Union Carbide, white workers, who were also farmers, received special privileges. Without losing seniority, white farmers were allowed to take sabbaticals in the spring and fall to plant and harvest crops. Blacks, as happened to Brookins, were often laid off in winter months when orders slowed, but whites continued to work throughout the year. When the AFL-CIO finally established a union at Union Carbide in 1951, the practice of allowing farmers to take off to tend to their fields was discontinued.[37] In the booming postwar years, Wood, Murphy, and Brookins did not have a difficult time finding a job. Rather, the difficulty was getting a job reflective of their skills and experience.

That unions could be an aid or a detriment to black workers could be seen in the creation of fair practices committees. The United Auto Workers (UAW) had as part of its constitution a provision for the establishment of fair practices committees in all locals. By 1949, only 39 of the 100 locals in Indiana and Kentucky had established such committees, even though UAW bylaws mandated them to do so.[38]

Faced with pressure from the national union to integrate membership, local unions found it easier simply to keep blacks out than to restrict their movement once employed. The technique most favored, and most effectively utilized, was to deny apprenticeship opportunities to African Americans. As mentioned previously with regard to African American veterans, blacks trained in segregated, usually ill-equipped facilities. When unions did ease restrictions to apprentice programs, many blacks were unable to exploit the newfound opportunities. An Indianapolis reporter noted in 1949 that it was "almost impossible for a Negro carpenter to get a union card here and only a few are in the bricklayers' union." Young men who somehow managed to serve apprenticeships were advised to go elsewhere, east or farther north, to practice their craft.[39] Only in the cement finishers, hod carriers, and common laborers locals were blacks in the majority, a circumstance that did not change for nearly twenty years. In conducting research for the Industrial Research Unit of The Wharton School of Business at the University of Pennsylvania on the opening of the building trade unions to African Americans, Richard L. Rowan and Lester Rubin found that many craft unions were made up almost exclusively of white males. (See Table 4.5) Of the 800 electricians registered in Indianapolis in 1970, only two were black. The situation was worse among Ironworkers and Sheet Metal Workers, who reported zero and one black member respectively.[40]

As was their practice, the NAACP, CIO, FAC, Jewish Federation, black newspapers across the state, and prominent individuals like Willard Ransom and Henry J. Richardson continued to pressure legislators and broaden their coalition. Reflecting a strong union presence, legislators from Gary and East Chicago were much more strident in their support for fair employment legislation than were representatives from Indianapolis. Perhaps as a matter of expediency and triage, Indianapolis representatives had their gaze fixed on the struggle to overcome school segregation, a problem that had been already resolved in the northern part of the state. But it is more likely that support from northern legislators testified to the strength of unions in that part of the state. In 1949, Indiana finally enacted a fair employment law, becoming one of the first states in the nation to adopt legislative measures for fair employment. Not uncharacteristically, however, compliance with the law was voluntary. Eight years after beginning the fight for fair employment legislation, supporters had reached a compromise that allowed them to claim victory. Previous disappointments, however, must have tempered their sense of accomplishment. One day after agreeing to the compromise, a reporter asked fair employment advocates if the recently adopted law would ease discrimination. They answered, "We hope so but doubt it."[41]

Under the agreement, a voluntary committee would present evidence to employers of the need for and efficacy of fair employment. The committee would then urge employers to hire and promote on the basis of merit and individual worth.[42] Agreeing to the compromise was a gamble for fair employment supporters. The new law did not attack the fundamental problems of job segregation or non-hiring. In fact, the new law did not help sympathetic personnel managers who would have preferred a law that forced their hand instead of one that gave them discretion. Black workers pointed to the law and told employers that African Americans "should" be hired, but white employees were equally justified in telling employers that they did not "have" to hire African Americans. Almost immediately, fair employment advocates reiterated their call for a fair employment law with teeth. Penalties alone, they argued, would force employers to follow the letter of the law.

The NAACP was even more forthcoming. The organization called the FEPC law "useless" and charged that the spirit and intent of the law was not being observed. Without significant penalties, the same odious practices would continue.[43] A *Recorder* editorial went even further; the fair employment law, it observed, was a "sham to no end forever."[44] The *Recorder* reiterated its call for es-

Table 4.5. Estimated Union Membership of Indianapolis Building Trades by Race

*African Americans encountered recalcitrant labor unions determined
to maintain homogeneity among their membership. Frequently the Locals
disregarded directives issued by their national body to diversity their membership.*

Craft	Estimated Membership March 1, 1970	Estimated number of Minorities March 1, 1970	Percent Minority
Asbestos Workers	222	0	0
Bricklayers	422	30	7.1
Carpenters	1,800	37	2.1
Cement Masons	200	140	70.0
Electricians	800	2	0.2
Elevator Constructors	120	2	1.7
Glaziers	87	2	2.3
Ironworkers	788	0	0
Lathers	100	1	1.0
Operating Engineers	1,200	42	3.5
Painters	366	0	0
Plasterers	95	8	8.4
Plumbers	362	7	1.9
Roofers	275	20	7.3
Sheet Metal Workers	650	1	0.2
Steamfitters	570	0	0
Tile & Marble Setters	120	5	4.2
Total	8,177	297	3.6

Source: Richard L. Rowan and Lester Rubin, *Opening the Skilled Construction Trade to Blacks* (Philadephia: University of Pennsylvania Press, 1972), 125. Although the term "minority" was used, blacks constituted over 98 percent of the non-white population in Marion County.

tablishment of an Urban League chapter, calling it a "crying need in Indianapolis." Editors and columnists recognized the work done by local groups but found them ineffective in the labor arena:

> We have outstanding civic organizations such as the NAACP, FAC, Flanner House, etc. The leaders and members have done a fine job. They have made many worthwhile contributions on the school front, civil rights, community improvement, and in the area of public health. Yet something is lacking. In the field of employment, Indianapolis Negroes have made few advances. But the question of jobs in industry and commerce is probably the most important of all. Working and earning a living is the central business of life from which everything flows.[45]

Economic challenges spurred intense discussion within the black community. For years there had been a thriving commercial and entertainment district along Indiana Avenue. Supported by the large number of blacks housed in Lockefield Gardens and the surrounding area, businesses thrived during the war and in the years shortly thereafter. By the 1950s, however, many small, black-owned businesses were failing because of insufficient clientele. Letters to the editor of the *Recorder* urged blacks to shop in stores that welcomed their presence and to avoid stores that treated them like second-class citizens or refused to hire them for jobs other than elevator operators or janitors. Reverend George Tate and the Progressive Civic League called upon people to help make jobs for the community. "We need to do like the Jews and be producers as well as consumers. Churches need to provide for social and economic betterment. African Americans need to start and own businesses."[46]

Andrew Ramsey, the longtime columnist for the *Recorder,* took an opposing position. Race pride in the form of solely patronizing black businesses was antithetical to American unity, he insisted. Blacks, Ramsey argued, could not demand first-class citizenship and simultaneously practice self-segregation. The solution, he believed, lay in fair employment. Making fair employment practices compulsory rather than voluntary would benefit the entire race instead of just the business class. Patronizing black-owned businesses benefited the businessperson; having fair, open hiring would benefit every working person. Pursuing the latter would in turn benefit black businesses.[47] This debate waxed and waned for more than a decade.

As stated above, labor unions had considerable influence over the types of jobs available to blacks. Frederick Kershner found that it was through labor movements that blacks took their first step toward economic equality in Indianapolis in the early years of the twentieth century.[48] However, labor unions were not as strong in Indianapolis as they were in other cities in the northern part of the state. They had their most encouraging success in the early decades of the twentieth century, when the city enjoyed a favorable business climate and was considered "a stronghold of organized labor," but their success was short-lived. In 1908, growing frustration over the establishment of the open shop erupted in violence when construction workers dynamited a work site. The incident ushered in a lasting distrust between unions and the larger community.[49]

By mid-century, the presence of labor unions was of little concern to African American workers. While the AFL-CIO steadfastly championed civil rights on the national level, its locals did little to bring about change in Indianapolis. White union officials admitted that when fair employment provisions were included in the locals' platform they were "almost always the first [issues] given up in negotiations."[50] By 1958, black workers at Allison had tired of petitioning their local's executive officers for fair and equitable treatment. A group of black workers wrote Walter Reuther, president of the UAW AFL-CIO, asking him to intercede on their behalf. The workers complained that "management and some of our officers are clearly doing many things to keep the Negro workers on just certain jobs, disregarding his seniority or ability." They highlighted incidents in which new workers were placed in positions that black workers had "bid" on previously. They also protested that Allison was not hiring enough blacks at any level. To their knowledge, only two black workers had been hired, even though the plant "had been doing a good deal of hiring."[51]

Personnel directors at factories had no interest in increasing the African American presence in the workforce and rarely placed blacks in positions traditionally held by whites. This policy, they argued, maintained peaceful and harmonious race relations. White employees, even union members, as shown by the situation at Allison, resisted efforts to include African Americans in either skilled or semi-skilled positions.[52] Either African Americans did not have the power to make white employers take them seriously, or they were easily placated. One of the most consistent themes expressed by readers of the *Recorder* was the ease with which certain members of the black community accepted scraps from the table rather than demanding a full meal. Andrew Ramsey consistently derided the community's apathy in fighting for a full measure of citizenship, although he must have known that various civil rights organizations were pressuring civic and industrial leaders. But flagging membership in the NAACP and a general acceptance of the status quo by most community members, Ramsey believed, reflected the community's indifference. The mechanisms were in place but people were not making full use of organizations or of their own collective strength. Fighting for change was a lonely endeavor, and Ramsey kept bumping into the same people along the battle lines.

In 1953, the legislature, seemingly bowing to external pressure, amended the FEPC act to prohibit any specification or discrimination as to race, creed, or ancestry on applications for employment. But whatever the amended act achieved was vitiated by a provision included by the framers that exempted applications requiring race, creed, or ancestral restrictions if "based upon a bona fide occupational qualification."[53]

With a legislature passing only toothless equal opportunity measures and with unions tacitly supporting discrimination in hiring and promotion, Indianapolis blacks were on their own. Fortunately, they maintained an informal but effective network of "getting on." One would be hard-pressed to view this network as a measure of resistance, but it did demonstrate the ways in which blacks coped with the prevailing system. Blacks knew which personnel directors were likely to hire them and which locals accepted their presence. It was not unusual for black workers to change jobs whenever opportunities presented themselves.[54] Lawrence Brookins used the informal network when he took a job at Union Carbide in 1946. "During that period there were just certain jobs that were open to blacks. Unless you knew someone who knew someone that could pull you in. Take Allison for instance. There were quite a few blacks working at Allison. But you had to know someone. The day that I went to Union Carbide I passed right by Allison. I passed right by because someone had told me they were hiring at Union Carbide."[55] But as effective as such a system might have been in getting friends and relatives employed, it did not expand the opportunities available to black workers as a whole. Merely obtaining a job was of such importance that other criteria, such as working conditions or union benefits, were rarely what pushed a black worker to accept a position. Lawrence Brookins recalled how people viewed job opportunities: "People during that time [1950s] . . . all they were interested in was a job. Whether it had a union or didn't have one the main issue was to get a job. Then maybe after they were there a while they could work to get a union in there."[56] Accordingly, one finds an incredible sameness to the work experiences of African Americans from decade to decade.

One element that influenced African American employment was industry's need for workers. For much of the 1950s and early 1960s, Indianapolis businesses experienced a labor shortage as the economy enjoyed almost full employment. By 1966, the unemployment rate hovered around 2.6 percent, only 0.6 percent above the "frictional unemployment" (the term given to full employment) rate of 2.0 percent.[57] Improved employment opportunities for blacks were not the result of corporate largess or successful moral persuasion by equal hiring advocates. Rather, blacks were employed because growth in the economy forced the hand of business. The advances they made in the workplace came because of the openings created by white abdication or corporate expansion. As pointed out in the discussion on housing, Indianapolis contractors could not build enough homes to keep up with frenzied demand. Apprenticeship programs were filled to capacity. Keeping blacks out of the buildings trades (as well as out of other units) effectively put the brakes on African American movement into more lucrative labor fields. It is tempting to examine statistics showing high black employment rates and to conclude that blacks were happily employed. The reality was that blacks were underemployed because effective barriers kept them in low-skilled industrial and craft positions while simultaneously blocking them from more profitable endeavors. It was not only the building trade unions that restricted black employment. As late as 1965, USS Corrugated Box Company still had an entire shift that included no African American workers.[58]

African Americans pushed for change and utilized the slow, evolutionary method of legislative reform. Resting their hopes on FEPC improvements and collaborative methods by AME and Flanner House, blacks missed out on the prosperous postwar economic boom. By the time legislators had strengthened the FEPC in the 1960s, it was too late. The economic boom, which lasted longer in Indianapolis than in many other cities, was over by 1971, the date generally accepted as the beginning of the depression in the local construction industry. White craftsmen now found themselves unemployed. In such a climate, blacks saw no reason to become involved in apprentice programs that had only recently begun accepting black students. Their decisions during the construction drought insured there would be few blacks prepared to enter the field when conditions improved.

Although their arguments had fallen on deaf ears, those who had pushed for more than thirty years for a stronger fair employment law had been correct. Without fear of reprisal, businesses employed discriminatory hiring and promotion practices throughout the 1960s. In his study of the implications of fair employment practices policies in Indianapolis in the 1960s, Stephen A. Wandner found that certain prevailing conditions controlled the labor market for African American males. At the most elemental level, Wandner found that the geographic location of firms within the standard metropolitan statistical area was an important determinant of the economic position of the black population. Central city segregation of the kind that plagued Indianapolis resulted in decreasing relative representation of blacks in firms located away from downtown. In other words, the farther the firm was from where blacks lived, the less likely it was to employ blacks. Black males were overrepresented in the labor force within the central city, underrepresented in the suburbs surrounding the central city at moderate distances, and highly underrepresented in firms located at greater distances from the city.[59]

For years, many African American commentators had argued that the fair employment laws were shams designed to give the appearance of fairness and equality without the power or intent to compel equity. Similar to the 1949 school law, fair employment statutes gave employers so much latitude that they were effectively free of obligation. Important allies of the Democratic Party, most notably the NAACP and the CIO, complained about the ineffectiveness of these laws. In 1960, they persuaded Matthew Welsh, the Democratic candidate for governor, to include in the party's platform a plank for stronger fair employment legislation. Welsh fulfilled his campaign debt by guiding the Civil Rights Act of 1961 through a stubborn General Assembly. The act promoted equal opportunity in employment and equal access to public accommodations. Under his guidance, the General Assembly created the Fair Employment Practice Act and the Indiana Civil Rights Commission (ICRC). The ICRC was to be the sole agency responsible for carrying out "the public policy of the State of Indiana to provide all of its citizens equal opportunity for employment." The Civil Rights Act empowered the ICRC to bring charges against a company or an industry practicing discriminatory hiring or promotion.[60]

The ICRC was responsible for monitoring corporate behavior regarding minority hiring and working conditions, and Harold Hatcher, a longtime civil rights advocate and former director of the Employment on Merit Program, a private organization initiated by the American Friends Service Committee, was named it first commissioner. Although Hatcher had been involved with fair employment concerns for some time, he was no radical. Perhaps in deference to Indiana's penchant for cautious, evolutionary change, but more likely out of recognition of the political clout of the Indiana Chamber of Commerce, which had strenuously objected to the ICRC's creation, Hatcher envisioned a commission that would work with corporations to establish unbiased hiring and promotion practices. Although endowed with the authority to file claims against offending corporations, Hatcher and the ICRC were not blessed with "cease and desist" enforcement powers. Even if the ICRC found a company guilty of discrimination, an event that rarely occurred in the 1960s, they were unable to impose a monetary fine, corrective measures, or any type of censure. Without the authority to issue cease and desist orders, they could note discriminatory practices but were unable to bring such practices to an end.[61]

In 1963, a change in Indiana law greatly strengthened the ICRC. Governor Welsh, solidly establishing himself as the Indiana governor who most aided African American workers, signed the Indiana Civil Rights Act of 1963, which replaced the Indiana Fair Employment Practice Act and supplanted the 1961 Civil Rights Act. Under the new law, the ICRC was given cease and desist enforcement powers. The new law, however, did not come without compromise. The Indiana Chamber of Commerce was able to restrict coverage to companies that employed more than five employees and, more importantly, eliminated the commission's power to initiate complaints as provided in the 1961 law. In other words, now that the commission had the power to stop illegal behavior, it was not free to initiate a complaint on workers' behalf. Individuals could file complaints for the ICRC to investigate, but discriminatory claims had to be brought by individual workers or job aspirants. Such a restriction inhibited the ICRC from instituting industry-wide reform even when they were aware of systemic, institutional discrimination. The 1963 law continued the practice of seeking a voluntary solution to any problems the commission encountered. Under Hatcher's guidance, the ICRC emphasized conciliation and cooperation between the commission and industry. There were only four hearings held and no cease and desist orders issued until 1969.

Hatcher argued that the 1963 law coerced the business community into complying with the commission's suggestions, thereby making cease and desist orders unnecessary.[62] But with no noticeable increase in work opportunities for aspiring African American construction workers or industry employees, it was evident that the 1963 law was either insufficient for the task or its application was ineffective. In 1969, legislators moved to attack both possibilities.

In 1969, the 1963 Indiana Civil Rights Act was amended with the addition of two important provisions that affected employment discrimination. The first

Chart 4.1. Complaints and Hearings of the Indiana Civil Rights Commission for the Entire State of Indiana, January 1, 1962, to June 30, 1971.

The Indiana Civil Rights Commission received consistent complaints from African American job seekers throughout the 1960s. However, it was not until 1970 that the Commission held hearings in significant number.

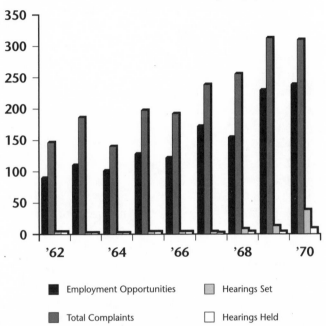

Employment Opportunities ■   Hearings Set ▨

Total Complaints ■   Hearings Held ☐

Stephen Arnold Wandner, "Racial Patterns of Employment in Indianapolis: The Implications for Fair Employment Practices Policy" (Ph.D. dissertation, Indiana University, 1972), 122.

was the addition of an enforceable consent agreement. The ICRC was instructed to encourage voluntary settlement of complaints of discrimination, but the terms of the settlement were to be stated in a written agreement, which had the same effect as a cease and desist order and could be enforced in circuit or superior courts. The second provision re-established ICRC-initiated complaints. The usual suspects, namely the Indiana Chamber of Commerce and other business interests, actively opposed the amendments in the General Assembly. This time a broad coalition, also familiar to the equal employment battle, was able to win enough support in the General Assembly to pass the legislation.[63]

In 1971, the law was further amended, with some implications for employment discrimination. The emphasis on voluntary agreement was eliminated, and the emphasis on discriminatory practices as an individual act was expanded to include "a system which excludes persons from equal opportunities." Finally, the ICRC could attack the industry discrimination that had plagued African Americans for decades.[64]

Harold Hatcher resigned from the ICRC in 1969 and was replaced by C. Lee Crean, a white Republican and longtime member of the Chamber of Commerce. Crean was much more confrontational than Hatcher. His personality, coupled with the added powers of the Civil Rights Act, allowed him to be far more aggressive in fighting discrimination.[65] Using the expanded Civil Rights Act, Crean initiated more discrimination hearings in eighteen months than Hatcher had overseen in the previous eight years.

In spite of these changes, the pattern of employment for Indianapolis's African Americans went unchanged. Between 1965 and 1970, only 14 percent of the complaints filed by black men were conciliated or adjusted. Most often, the company promised to take remedial action without admitting guilt. Furthermore, the more than 10,000 black male workers in Indianapolis had filed only 331 complaints. Most black workers seemed to believe that possible reprisals greatly outweighed any advantages they might have received from a favorable hearing.[66]

Equal employment advocates finally had the law they had long sought, but it came too late. Indianapolis's advocates had preached voluntary, conciliatory mediation while simultaneously working to strengthen state laws prohibiting worker discrimination, but they were fighting with worn-out weapons. The piecemeal benefits won were effectively useless in improving the day-to-day job conditions of African Americans and in providing access to apprentice programs and high-paying union jobs. Nonetheless, this approach might have been successful in staving off white community unrest—a goal long advocated by employers. Consequently, the one-note song sung by African American workers in 1941 was still being hummed in 1970. African Americans worked, but the jobs they held and the opportunities they encountered were governed by the racism prevailing in Indianapolis.

5

Building a Fence around the City
African Americans and Unigov

In each of the previous areas of analysis—education, labor, and housing—a familiar pattern of black protest was readily apparent. Through petition or direct appeal, representatives of the black community, most often institutions or organizational leaders, would beseech white officials to address an area of concern. If rebuffed, which was all too often the case, blacks would continue to press for reform while simultaneously enlarging their coalition to include white citizens of "conscience." If their appeals failed, as they so frequently did, then those same representatives sought legislative or court remedies. At best, such approaches were slow, tedious forms of protest whose most salient benefit was rather harmonious relations between the black and white communities. At worst, such strategies delayed reform until the objectives—open housing, school integration, job diversification—no longer matched current inequalities.

Throughout the time period under study, the black community and the Democratic Party solidified their relationship. One of the results of their relationship was that by 1968 Democrats had occupied the mayor's office for twenty-eight of the previous forty years. But although the Democratic Party was successful at the polls, African Americans were not nearly as successful in reaping the benefits of their long association. Yet as the Democratic Party solidified its hold on many important elected positions, it became less feasible for blacks to divorce themselves from the party (a move that risked their becoming politically irrelevant) than it was to continue the marriage and work (hope) for better days.

But it was not that the days were that bad—at least not statistically. To many, Indianapolis blacks were a model community. When compared to nearby African American communities in Chicago, Cincinnati, Detroit, and St. Louis, African Americans in Indianapolis had the highest level of home ownership, educational attainment, and per capita income. That the homes were sometimes substandard, the jobs too frequently menial, and the schooling of uneven quality is apparent from reading the previous chapters. Nevertheless, the progress the community had made led sufficient numbers of African Americans to support protracted reform by way of interracial political negotiations.

However good or bad were African American fortunes, the situation changed dramatically in 1969. Members of the white community had often tried to limit African American mobility in the housing and labor markets, all in an attempt to preserve an Indianapolis that was favorable to their interests. In many instructive ways, these efforts culminated in the enactment of Unified Government (Unigov) in 1969. Perhaps no other single event demonstrates the many issues that characterized the political economy of race in the city. Community apathy, private cartels, behind-the-scenes deals, political impotency, disunity, and second-class citizenship are all to be found in the history of Unigov. It was truly Indianapolis's own creation.

The situation did not look so bleak at the beginning of the decade. Democrats looked to decentralize the city government and fortify their already formidable hold on the mayor's office. African Americans believed that what was good for the Democratic Party was good for them, too. John Barton, Democratic mayor from 1963 to 1967, and James W. Beatty, Marion County Democratic chair and corporate counsel of Indianapolis, believed that government reorganization was the key to the city's survival. In 1964, shortly after Barton's election, Beatty sponsored a reorganization of Indianapolis's governmental structure. Barton supported Beatty because he was frustrated with the executive office's inability to control the semi-autonomous agencies and boards that controlled most local and county functions. By 1967, the Census of Governments recorded sixty governments within Marion County: the county, twenty-three cities and towns, nine townships, eleven school districts, and sixteen special-purpose governments.[1]

Barton may have been Beatty's ally, but Barton was not nearly as revolutionary. Hoping to take advantage of the 1964 election, which seated a Democratic governor and mayor as well as Democratic majorities in both houses of the Indiana General Assembly, the Marion County state legislative delegation, and the Indianapolis City Council, Beatty proposed a series of fourteen related bills that, if adopted, would have greatly strengthened the mayor's office.[2] Beatty's proposal stopped there. Democrats were not as perturbed by the exodus to the suburbs as were their Republican counterparts, for white, middle-class migration from the central city greatly enhanced Democratic chances at elections.[3] Beatty's goal was to strengthen the mayor's office by increasing administrators' loyalty and dependence on the mayor. Significantly, Beatty did not propose altering the agencies' basic structure or jurisdiction; rather, he merely wanted the mayor to have authority to appoint board members.

It is likely that Beatty never anticipated the maelstrom that met his proposed changes. First, he greatly underestimated the power of the media. The *Indianapolis Star* and *News,* both owned by the Pulliam organization, assailed the consolidation as a "power grab," a term that stuck. With the newspapers leading the way, criticism followed from the affected agencies and the Republican Party. Agency leaders argued that boards would lose autonomy and become puppets of the city administration. Republicans alleged that the Democrats wanted to reinforce their stranglehold on the mayor's office, an office Democrats had won in seven of the previous nine elections, largely through patronage. Beatty could have held off agency leaders and Republicans, but the newspapers were relentless in their criticism. Barton, never strongly in favor of the attempt, began to waver and indicted Beatty for creating the mess, saying, "Most of the bills . . . were being promoted by the Democratic organization, not the city administration."[4]

Beatty doggedly presented the proposals to the General Assembly, where he made his second blunder. He erroneously assumed that Democrats in the General Assembly would support local Democratic initiatives as a matter of course. Consequently, he did not sufficiently strengthen his coalition or make enough people aware of his plans. Although blessed with an abundance of office holders, Democrats were not able to capitalize on their good fortune. Members of the state assembly were ill prepared to face the media onslaught over a proposal they only vaguely understood. The local coalition was equally ill prepared. The General Assembly largely rejected Beatty's reorganization plan when they defeated nine of the fourteen bills presented for their consideration. Nothing symbolized the fractured Democratic relationships more than the split between Barton and Beatty. Barton, representing the "old guard," and Beatty, the "young Turks," eventually made their fight public when the two faced off in the 1967 Democratic primary. Barton won, but the fight weakened the Democrats and left them susceptible to a Republican challenge.

On the national level, Republicans experienced a change of fortune in 1967 and 1968, largely because voters were tired of the seemingly endless Vietnam War, unrest in urban centers, and incessant and increased demands by civil rights organizations. Indiana voters sent Republican majorities to both houses of the General Assembly and seated a Republican governor. Indianapolis was quiet relative to some of its northern neighbors, but those with a sensitive ear could hear the grumbling emanating from an African American population tired of tokenism and waiting for "100 per cent citizenship." Some community leaders warned that good and peaceful race relations could end if demonstrable progress was not forthcoming.[5] Republicans swept to office in the charged political environment and controlled all the important state offices, both houses of the General Assembly, and virtually every vital post in Indianapolis, including the mayor's office, won by Dick Lugar. Blessed with the same opportunity Democrats had enjoyed four years earlier, Lugar and his Republican cohorts did not waste their good fortune.

During the mayoral campaign, Lugar offered few specifics concerning government reorganization.[6] Instead, his campaign rhetoric centered on school reform, increased application for federal funds, and dynamic leadership. The last pledge might have contained a veiled hint at the revolutionary changes he had in mind, but it was widely interpreted to refer to his youthful energy. Lugar was thirty-five years old when he assumed the mayor's office in 1968. His age belied the experience he brought to the job. A local son, Lugar was valedictorian of his graduating class at Shortridge High School. He won Phi Beta Kappa honors at Denison University, where he was also first in the class of 1954. He was Denison's first Rhodes Scholar and studied politics, philosophy, and economics at Pembroke College, Oxford. After a three-year stint in the Navy, Lugar returned to Indianapolis to revitalize the family businesses. He also involved himself in local politics and in 1964 was elected to the embattled Indianapolis school board.[7]

Unigov was Dick Lugar's brainchild, and he utilized a combination of immense political skill, fortuitous timing, and solid organization to gain its acceptance. But although Dick Lugar introduced Unigov to Indianapolis, the concept was hardly original. In the 1930s, political scientists and good government groups advocated schemes for integrating and coordinating the activities of local governments in metropolitan areas.[8] By mid-century, a few southern cities, Nashville–Davidson County, Jacksonville–Duval County, and Baton Rouge–East Baton Rouge Parish, had executed consolidations in 1963, 1968, and 1949 respectively. In all, by 1972, eighteen municipalities operated under city-county consolidation.[9] Lugar worked tirelessly to bring his vision to fruition. After his mayoral victory, he traveled the "mashed potato circuit" to help Republican candidates gain statewide office. When Unigov reached the General Assembly, Lugar had many favors owed him.

Anyone who questions Indianapolis's distinctiveness need look no further than Unigov, the political system that has ordered Indianapolis government since 1969. Unigov consolidated the policy-making structures of the city and the county, with the notable exception of school systems and fire and police services. Indianapolis was not the first city in the country to adopt a unified structure, but it was the first northern city so constructed in the twentieth century, and it was the first since New York City underwent consolidation in 1897 to do so without a public referendum.[10]

In the view of Dick Lugar, Indianapolis was like a root-bound plant. City and county administrative offices often had overlapping jurisdiction and duplication of services. For instance, there were twenty-four different police units operating in Marion County. The state, city, county, and a township shared airport operations. Five separate governmental entities constructed and maintained highways, streets, and bridges. Frequently, administrators of city and county departments were not answerable to the mayor but rather to a board that oversaw the departments' functions. Lugar cited the various centers of power as examples of an "archaic, expensive and overlapping Model-T form of government."[11] The system, Lugar argued, inhibited growth and choked off any meaningful reform efforts. Lugar championed county leadership in private discussions with President Richard Nixon and in public to the national association of county officials in 1969.[12]

One of the most consistent criticisms lodged against Unigov is its effect on the African American population. Critics, mostly Democrat, have complained that the Republicans' true intent with Unigov was to secure suburban, largely white Republican voters while purposely diluting the political clout of African American votes. In Unigov's creation, one sees how policies have traditionally been implemented and how politically impotent the black population was. Unigov may have been a fight for political power between Republicans and Democrats, but its deployment had a dramatic effect on the African American community.

Unigov was not the first structural change in government that diminished black voting power in Indianapolis. Near the turn of the twentieth century, business and political leaders had championed an at-large voting system that had also diluted the African American vote. Constrained into identifiable wards, African Americans were unable to elect representatives who focused on their needs, though it was not uncommon for a black member to sit on the city council. Indeed, by the 1960s it was a common occurrence for an African American to be on the council. The existing elective structure called for each party to nominate six candidates for the city council. It was customary for each party to nominate five white candidates and one African American. Each voter had the opportunity to cast nine votes. Making up nearly 27 percent of the city's population in 1960, African Americans were such an important voting constituency that both the Republicans and Democrats usually included one African American among their slate of candidates.[13] The winning party would seat all of its candidates, and the three highest vote getters of the opposing party would be seated on the council. The losing party would rarely seat a black candidate because a black candidate would rarely be one of the top three vote getters.

In addition to reforming government, Republicans were interested in improving their political fortunes. Like most northern industrial cities, Indianapolis had begun to lose population in the 1950s and early 1960s as more and more citizens opted for suburban living. The exodus was particularly distressing for city officials because the émigrés took valuable tax revenues with them. Republican politicians were particularly concerned because many of the émigrés were Republican. Faced with a decreased tax base, Indianapolis could not afford to undertake the expensive urban renewal necessary to attract new residents or entice corporations to relocate to the city. Reform had to accomplish the seemingly contradictory task of increasing the number of Republican voters and centralizing government operations.

Lugar was a founding member of the Republican Action Committee (RAC), whose members were stung by the party's sweeping electoral defeat in 1964 and who were dedicated to replacing the old guard with a group of young, active, reform-oriented leaders. The RAC wrested control of the Republican Party and seated one of their own, L. Keith Bulen, former member of the General Assembly, as county party chairman. The RAC was also instrumental in getting their nominees elected and in centralizing party power. Perhaps more importantly, the RAC demonstrated how a committed, focused minority could challenge established practices. Lugar and the RAC used the same strategy in creating Unigov.[14]

Within two months of Lugar's election, Republicans created a "kitchen cabinet" composed of: Beurt SerVaas, president of the Marion County Council and a businessman; John Burkhart, president of the College Life Insurance Company; Thomas C. Hasbrook, an executive in the Eli Lilly Company; John Walls, chief staff officer of the Greater Indianapolis Progress Committee; state Senator Lawrence M. Borst, a veterinarian and chair of Marion County's legislative delegation; and Charles L. Whistler, president of the Metropolitan Planning Commission. This group, later known as the policy committee, created the general structure of Unigov.[15] The group's explicit purpose was to compose a draft for government reorganization. That the committee formed so quickly after Lugar's inauguration suggests the extent to which the overlapping, duplicative nature of Indianapolis's and Marion County's governing bureaucracy bothered Republicans.[16] Like the Democrats, the policy committee believed the structure to be horribly inefficient. The quick formation also testified to how serious the Republicans were and how prepared they were to wrest control from the Democratic Party.

With Dick Lugar in attendance, the policy committee met at John Burkhart's house every Sunday for nine months in 1968. At these informal meetings the participants crafted Unigov. They left its final form to a team of lawyers, but it was the committee that provided the framework. In creating the proposal behind closed doors, the committee was able to avoid the public scrutiny that had destroyed the Democrats' plans. But what really separated the committee's efforts from those of the Democrats was its inclusion of city, county, state, and business interest representatives. By including so many constituency representatives around the dining room table, the committee garnered considerable support before its proposals were made public.[17]

However complete their plans, the policy committee realized they could not present their reorganization plan to the public without first widening their coalition. The creation of the mayor's task force solved that problem.[18] But while the group's existence gave the appearance of openness and flexibility, Hasbrook and SerVaas's role as co-chairs underscored the continuing influence of the policy committee. Mayor Lugar detailed the task force's responsibilities in the letter inviting members to serve on the committee. The members were to direct preparation of legislation for presentation to the 1969 General Assembly by a committee of lawyers who prepared the actual bill, work with members of the General Assembly and the public in promoting the legislative program, and give guidance to the mayor and other public officials in establishing the governmental structure following a successful legislative effort.[19] The task force's most important contribution was its sanctioning of Unigov. The policy committee had carefully and wisely selected members of the community who could act as ambassadors for Unigov during the legislative battle. In so doing, Republicans were able to assert to state legislators that Unigov was a community-sanctioned endeavor, a claim the Democrats could not make in 1964.

In truth, few Indianapolis citizens had a clear idea of what Unigov promised. The Indianapolis Jaycees conducted a phone survey to gauge the public's attitude concerning Unigov. On Valentine's Day 1969, the Jaycees phoned 2,800 households selected at random. To offer their opinion, respondents had to be at least twenty-one years old, reside at the household selected, and have a familiarity with the Unigov proposal. The last criterion removed most citizens from consideration. In the end, only 281 people (19 percent) met the requirements. Of those, 69 percent of the respondents favored the adoption of Unigov.[20] Obviously, the most noteworthy aspect of the survey was the large number of people not allowed to respond. With all the significant work done behind closed doors and participation limited by invitation, it should have come as no surprise that few citizens had a clear idea of Unigov's particulars. The RAC had no incentive to educate the populace. Popular support was welcome, but it was clearly not necessary. Because the reorganization plan would not undergo a public referendum, the only support needed for enactment was that of elected officials. The RAC effectively gathered support from elected officials and well-placed community leaders. In Indiana, with no "home rule" tradition, these efforts were sufficient. Unigov was possible only because Indianapolis did not enjoy home rule.[21] The state of Indiana had complete legal authority over Indianapolis's government structure and powers, and it dictated how the city was organized. Most importantly, the General Assembly had the power to change the city's governmental structure without first seeking a constitutional amendment or holding a local referendum. Most observers agreed that due largely to the number and effectiveness of African American voting and Democratic Party organization, Unigov supporters would not have been able to enact their proposals had there been a referendum.[22]

Republicans received assistance from numerous respected community entities. On February 7, 1969, the League of Women Voters sent a statement to the Joint Committees of the Indiana General Assembly on Affairs of Marion County asserting that they were "strong supporters" of metropolitan government because "we believe it is the most efficient way to govern and because it offers the best value for the taxpayer." The League of Women Voters argued that the current organization was too confusing. The Greater Indianapolis Progress Committee, the 400-member organization of city leaders working for the development of Indianapolis, "strongly endorsed the proposal for government unification." The beat continued with the Indianapolis Real Estate Board, the Indianapolis Civic Progress Association, the Jaycees, and the Chamber of Commerce all sending statements in support of Unigov to the Indiana General Assembly. Local radio and television outlets offered editorials clarifying and supporting Unigov.[23] Although Unigov gave unprecedented power to the mayor, who had political leadership over most government activities in the city through his powers to appoint department leaders, this circumstance apparently did not concern media commentators as it had done four years before as part of the Democratic Party's reorganization proposal.[24]

The Indianapolis reorganization bill went before the Indiana General Assembly with the full support of the Marion County delegation. At public hearings held to gauge popular sentiment for reorganization, disparate groups, made up of ultraconservatives, blacks, and the Democratic Party, stood in opposition.[25] Conservatives, some believed to be members of the John Birch Society, argued that the Republicans were attempting to create a virtual dictatorship and a front for Communist initiatives. As comical as some of the conservatives' claims were, at least they were united in their condemnation of Unigov. The same could not be said for liberal coalitions. Labor leaders stood against Unigov and criticized the absence from the plan of police, fire departments, and schools. But when pressed to provide evidence of their members' feelings concerning reorganization, leaders were forced to admit they had none.[26] The Indiana Conference on Civil and Human Rights (ICCHR) was concerned about the exclusion of schools and the possibility of gerrymandered council districts. The ICCHR was most disturbed by the disregard paid the Mayor's Commission on Human Rights, likening its positioning within the Unigov organizational hierarchy to that of a "seemingly unwanted stepchild."[27] They vowed not to support Unigov until significant revisions were made, and on February 24, 1969, they demonstrated their commitment to defeating Unigov by marching on the state legislature. The Central Christian Leadership Council (CCLC), led by its president, Reverend Joe Turner, charged the Unigov bill with "discrimination, partiality, and prejudice." The CCLC promised to file suit with the state supreme court. Rev. Turner believed there to be more compelling reasons for Republican support of Unigov than an effort to improve government efficiency.

If Unigov passed, he alleged, "Prejudice minded whites will not have to solicit black votes . . . the white power structure is attempting to build a fence around the city."[28]

African American leaders, at least those who commented, uniformly rejected Unigov, but their opposition was to no avail. Perhaps more significantly, there was little coordination between the groups and institutions opposed to Unigov. Frank P. Lloyd, a prominent black physician and influential Democratic Party member, explained:

> There was just no black leadership in this community. Blacks are just not organized at all. And, if you looked at blacks in the community, we were divided even on that. For example, I certainly am not against Unigov. But I would prefer that the schools be under Unigov. I was part of the Democratic try to get the police and fire metropolitanized for the very simple reason that I wanted to extend the tax base.[29]

The *Indianapolis Recorder,* perhaps reflecting both the fear and disharmony among African Americans, could only use the phrase "Negro community" to refer to voices of protest. Editors quoted "spokesmen" without attribution. Evidently, the sources the editors quoted were unwilling to have their names associated with their statements. In editorials, the *Recorder* identified some of the more worrisome features of Unigov. Republicans made a great deal of the value that single-member districts, which would supplant the existing at-large format, would offer to African American neighborhoods, but commentators pointed out that nowhere in Unigov's proposal were council districts specified. There was a great fear in the black community that districts would be drawn to minimize the possibility of black participation on the city council. Attorney Henry J. Richardson, Jr. spoke for some when his letter to the editor, published in the *Recorder,* argued that the real impetus behind Unigov was to eliminate the likelihood of the city ever electing a black mayor. Quoting unnamed sources, Richardson accused the mayor's advisors and supporters of the bill of saying to white audiences, "We must have this legislation to prevent Indianapolis from becoming another Gary," a direct reference to Richard Hatcher's recent victory in Gary's mayoral election. Andrew Ramsey, *Recorder* columnist, probably put it best when he wrote:

> The local Republican Party which has done little to woo the black vote is now out to eliminate the need of it in the future. . . . It is not surprising therefore, that in the controversy centering around Mayor Richard Lugar's plan to dilute the black vote and to render ineffectual the local black vote in the future, Negroes cannot count on either the liberals, the Jews, the Catholics or the white Protestants. By far and large they are for the plan no matter what it does to Sepia Indianapolis. So here, in Indianapolis, the Negro needs friends as he does nationally. The sixty four dollar question is "where to find them?"[30]

By 1970, African Americans were a numerical majority of the population in sixteen American cities. In fourteen additional cities, the black population exceeded 43 percent. Black political strategists and activists welcomed the emergence of cities with black majorities and the prospect of achieving political liberation through the most basic democratic means: numerical superiority.[31]

Patrick E. Chavis, Jr., an African American and former state senator from Indianapolis, may have offered the most tangible evidence of the motives behind Unigov. Chavis had initially offered qualified support of Unigov because it promised to extend municipal enforcement of open housing to the county as a whole. That fact alone was sufficient to guarantee Chavis's initial support. Less than a week after Chavis's comments appeared in the press, Unigov was amended. Chavis took note:

> No sooner than my statement was made the whole Lugar Machine snapped to attention and amended the bill, now county residents will not be subjected in any way to the enforcement of city ordinances. The insidious five ordinances which have long been used to harass black citizens in their homes and clubs will still be applicable to city residents while county residents will be immune.[32]

Chavis then urged blacks to fight against Unigov because the proposed system of government would give black citizens a "double standard of law enforcement, one which is calculated to destroy our confidence in its motive and perpetuate unfair and unequal treatment of the citizens of the inner city."[33] Chavis did not share the views of political scientists who criticized the Democrats' inability to garner support for their reform efforts. Chavis believed it was the threat that Indianapolis would mimic Gary and Cleveland that led the Republicans to be successful where the Democrats had failed.

The Democratic organization was aware of the potential danger Unigov presented to their electoral chances. They quickly cried foul and charged that Republicans were hypocritically following a course they had decried four year earlier when the Democrats had attempted reorganization. Of particular concern to Democrats was the weakening of their political strength. Blacks consistently voted for Democratic candidates in Indianapolis, and more importantly they voted in significant numbers. African American political participation in Indianapolis, as measured by the levels of registration and voting, equaled that of whites, irrespective of socioeconomic status or income and educational levels. When controlled for socioeconomic status, African Americans tended to participate more actively in politics than did whites.[34] Yet Democrats could not band together to forestall Unigov. James Beatty was in a difficult position. He had authored legislation four years earlier designed to eliminate the gridlock and duplication running rampant in Marion County. The Unigov proposal, while not providing sweeping social reform, did address issues Beatty had promoted.

Democrats in the General Assembly took their cue from the Marion County organization and were equally ambivalent. Something about Unigov was unsettling, but politicians were unable to fashion their discomfort into a coordinated, effective rebuke of Republican efforts. Most recognized the political implications of rejecting a measure that closely resembled one Democrats had supported four years earlier. Most legislators saw Unigov as a problem for Marion County and not for the state as a whole. To their credit, however, political parties learned their lesson when similar reorganizations plans arose closer to home. When reformers proposed change for Evansville and South Bend, the party most likely to suffer long-term harm rose quickly and successfully to defeat reorganization.[35]

In the end, Unigov easily sailed through the General Assembly because Republicans at various levels consistently supported the initiative. Traditionally, state representatives acquiesced to the wishes of county delegations when proposed legislation affected only that district. Marion County representatives were consistent and firm in their support. Lugar made the short trip from his office to the state legislature to lobby for support. He tirelessly explained the nuances of Unigov and quieted members' fears about a popular revolt against Unigov. Lugar and the RAC had effectively shored up their support. They had even placated the *Indianapolis News* and *Indianapolis Star,* who were early opponents of the reorganization plan. Republicans were also greatly aided by the divided Democratic Party. Although Republicans held majorities in the General Assembly, Lugar needed Democratic support to pass the bill. As had occurred on the local level, Democrats, largely caught off guard, could not muster a coordinated effort to defeat passage of the bill. Governor Edgar C. Whitcomb signed Unigov into law on March 13, 1969.[36]

The media attempted to make the 1971 mayoral election a referendum on Unigov. Lugar campaigned on the issue while his Democratic opponent, John Neff, criticized Unigov for being a tool of the Republican Party and a reform effort that did not truly and progressively alter the structure of government in Indianapolis. The centerpiece of his criticism was the absence of police, fire departments, and school systems from the Unigov system. Neff had a difficult juggling act to accomplish. To win the election he had to court the conservative suburban voters now eligible to vote in the Indianapolis mayoral contest while also satisfying the large black voting contingent in the central city. He chose to attract white votes by warning that Unigov would mean open housing and busing of suburban schoolchildren to inner-city schools, and he chose to risk alienating African American voters, trusting that their commitment to the Democratic Party would remain firm.

Neff's "picket fence" campaign, so dubbed because of campaign literature depicting a picket fence under a caption which read "Neff for your Neighborhood," was a disaster. Dr. Frank Lloyd, a prominent black Democrat, attacked his party's choice for mayor and accused Neff of not so subtly implying that a vote for him was a vote to keep blacks out of their suburban neighborhoods.[37] Neff's association with Ja Neen Welsh also significantly hurt him. Welsh had campaigned with Alabama governor George C. Wallace during his unsuccessful bid for president in 1968. At the time, Welsh had suggested that she and Wallace were romantically involved. Neff and Welsh appeared together in suburban newspaper advertisements, and her mere presence did more to hurt Neff's support in the black community than anything Lugar said or did. African Americans questioned the judgment and commitment of a mayoral candidate who associated with someone who had had a relationship with Wallace, the segregationist governor of Alabama. Neff's controversial campaign strategy and his continued involvement with Welsh led some black members of the Democratic Party to write, "[Neff's campaign] is a direct slap in the face of every thinking black member of this community."[38]

Editors at the *Recorder* were so stung by Neff's platform and campaign strategy that they unabashedly urged black voters to vote for Lugar instead of a candidate that was clearly taking them for granted.[39] Lugar won the election in a landslide. Some political scientists have interpreted the black vote for Lugar as an endorsement of Unigov.[40] The evidence suggests, however, that the African American vote for Lugar was a vote against Neff. Lugar and Neff may have run their campaigns around the Unigov issue, but to most African Americans, as well as most of the city's white residents, Unigov was already a *fait accompli.*

The RAC claimed that reorganization would bring increased efficiency, centralization, and growth. Researchers William Blomquist and Roger Parks argue that Unigov has failed in its stated mission to create a more efficient urban organization, and that "the extent to which Unigov simplified local public service delivery is arguable." While Marion County retains fifty separate local governments (down from sixty in 1967), the number of separate taxing units in the county has grown since 1970 to approximately 100. In some respects, the Unigov structure is even more complicated than that which it replaced.[41] Reorganization, however, had successfully turned a traditionally Democratic stronghold into a bastion of Republican office holding. Robert Voss Kirch's pronouncement in 1973 now appears prophetic. In a paper delivered before the Indiana Academy of Sciences, Kirch closed his remarks on the political implication of Unigov by saying, ". . . it would appear that Indianapolis will continue to be referred to as the largest city in the nation with a Republican mayor and administration for many, many years to come."[42]

In 1960, African Americans constituted nearly 27 percent (130,000 persons) of the city's population. The combination of white flight from Center Township, which held nearly two-thirds of the city's population, and the continued growth of the black community led some demographers to project that blacks would make up between 30 and 40 percent of the population by 1970. Under Unigov, the incorporation of the mostly white suburbs dropped the African American presence in the city to 18 percent, and black political strength reverted to levels reached in 1945.[43] Just as Cleveland and Gary were electing black mayors, Indianapolis blacks were watching their political strength diminish. By 1973, Henry J. Richardson, longtime activist and community leader, had seen enough. His resignation from the GIPC summed his feelings about a lifetime of trying to better race relations and civil rights in Indianapolis:

> I have concluded that my contributions have not been constructively necessary and beneficial and has meant little to the development of the human personality of our community. As I reflect over a period of 50 years of public life, I feel that there is more ill will and strife in our community now than during the Klan days. This proves to me definitely that fundamentally as a matter of human rights and justice, we have made no progress in this community, and my contributions have been isolated, token cells of fragmented progress motivated largely by expediency. The basic political, social and economic mores of this community are still bullishly controlled and directed by selfishness and deep racial prejudices maintained by bullish status quo procrastinators. The moral and ethical context of equal opportunity and options for all citizens alike does not exist—and is prohibited by the maintainers of the status quo through the economic, political and social, power-control cells of Indianapolis. I wish to tender my resignation from the GIPC.[44]

Any assessment of black political strength in Indianapolis is open to much debate. Republicans have pointed to Unigov's eradication of citywide representation on the city council and the construction of single-member districts as the provision that has significantly increased black representation on the city council. In the last pre-Unigov election in 1967, only one black councilman was elected to the nine-member city council. Under the old system described earlier, each party nominated six candidates for the city council, and it was customary for each party to nominate five white and one African American candidate. The old system had fulfilled its first goal, the elimination of ward bosses, but replaced it with political party bosses. Black candidates then had first to curry favor with the political party because it was the party that constructed the candidate list. There was no particular reason for black candidates to pursue an agenda favorable to the black community because community support did not guarantee inclusion on the party's list of candidates. Unigov, however, promised to make council members responsible to their districts. Consequently, many people were understandably in a quandary over which system most benefited the black community. Under Unigov, the percentage of black candidates seated on the county council has increased; however, since most black council members have been Democrats on a council dominated by Republicans, their influence is debatable.[45] Democrats have consistently derided Unigov as a system that has uniformly produced Republicans majorities.

Another of the lessons from Unigov is not quite so murky. The organizations that African Americans had created and maintained for decades were clearly unprepared to challenge Unigov. Long independent, they were unable to form a coalition that could ably stand in the way of Lugar's organized reform effort. In every major fight against housing, labor, and education discrimination, blacks formed biracial coalitions to press for reform. That strategy had its limits, for when an issue like Unigov worked solely against the black community, biracial coalitions were difficult to form. The Democratic Party could have provided a forum, but they had neglected the African American community and taken it for granted. Despite their numbers, African Americans were unable to defeat legislation detrimental to their interests.

Tracking political influence and representation is dangerous territory for a historian, especially in a city like Indianapolis where so much discussion and drafting of legislation was done behind closed doors. It is more worthwhile to evaluate the process and the goals, both intended and unintended, by which change takes place. In a city and state well known for incremental and evolutionary change, it is startling to find two major alterations of city government within the same century. Andrew Ramsey summed up his perspective on Unigov and black participation in city affairs when he wrote, "We had already lost when Unigov was crammed down our throats by the 1969 General Assembly and the political muscle of Keith Bulen and Richard Lugar . . . many blacks who uttered no protest when it was being hatched now see that they have been had."[46] It is the frustration one feels after being duped that fuels much of the mistrust found in the black community. Unigov was efficiently and legally enacted, but many share Ramsey's sentiment that a group that had definite political and social goals sprang it on an unsuspecting populace. Instead of uniting a city and county, it widened the gulf between the African American and white communities. Masterfully orchestrated by Lugar, the Unigov campaign demonstrated how politically impotent the black community was and how removed their leaders were from the halls of power. Their criticisms of Unigov had no noticeable effect on the outcome. There were no African Americans gathered around John Burkhart's dining room table as the city's reorganization plan was drafted. The framers of one of the most sweeping government reorganizations in a century did not need an African American in their midst in order to carry out their agenda. That may be the most telling legacy of Unigov and Indianapolis's political power.

It may be that a future historian studying Indianapolis will list Unigov as just another obstacle blacks had to overcome in order to obtain full citizenship. Since before World War II, African Americans have had to pull down walls protecting the bastion of segregation. As the century progressed, the incidences of racism became subtler. Each of the previous chapters details how the larger community reacted to the black community's challenge. Often the efforts of the black community to end segregation slowly brought about desegregation, but rarely did real progress follow.

Conclusion

One of the enduring precepts of those who question the long-standing impact of African American struggles undertaken during the twentieth century is that African Americans were too impatient. American officials as well-known as President Dwight Eisenhower and as obscure as Judge John L. Niblack have uttered the familiar phrase "not now, but soon," to assuage persistent African American demands for political redress. Protests and aggressive legal challenges, they argued, only worked to harden opposition to integration of the races. Patience, they believed, would allow whites and African Americans to familiarize themselves with each other, and eventually there would be no need for legal remedy because people would move together of their own accord. The bulk of this book makes such an argument appear simplistic and fallacious. White residents in Indianapolis did not support political leaders who maintained segregation because these residents were unfamiliar with their African American neighbors. They did so because racial segregation upheld their vested economic and political interests. That segregation also resonated with racists is obvious, yet to argue that racism, alone or primarily, brought segregation ignores the structural composition of the city. Accordingly, Indianapolis's African Americans attacked the structures because segregation was a much more significant problem than was racism. The style of protest they employed, as I demonstrated in the preceding chapters, was developed with recognition of local realities. Yet their polite and patient protest met with interminable delays and ineffectual remedies.

Yet even though one may criticize the impact of their protests, African American actions should not be dismissed. For too long, we have left unchallenged the notion that African American protest needed the accompaniment of mass demonstration. African Americans in Indianapolis realized that large-scale public demonstrations were out of character and potentially counterproductive. If we are to truly understand the experiences of those who lived in the cities we study, then we must be cognizant of the structural realities they encountered and challenged. In addition to analyzing their protest efforts, I have included quality of life measures that will enable scholars to make comparisons across region and time. Clearly, I am not dismissive of the protest strategies of Indianapolis's African American community, but I remain critical of their choices because they were unable to increase their fortune significantly. Their strategies were better suited to maintaining the gains they had made before segregation became firmly entrenched. As the wall of segregation was more securely established, African American protest efforts were less successful. In the end, the establishment of Unigov deprived them of the strength that their numerical presence promised.

In using race as a component of the political economy, race becomes one factor among many that competed in the urban arena. Undoubtedly, economic agents, whether they were real estate brokers or industrial and political leaders, used race to encourage specific constituencies. Race had a currency, and its value fluctuated in accordance with the number of African Americans and the loci of their protest efforts. Race, then, was a variable in the political economy. Real estate brokers hinted at the reduced value white-owned homes would have if African Americans moved into the neighborhood; when pushing for Unigov, politicians hinted at the specter of a power structure determined by African American voters. In each case, and in others found throughout this book, white leaders responded to the increased African American presence by creating structures to contain them or reduce their political value.

African Americans recognized the political economy at work and diligently tried to form coalition partners. Their miscalculation was in failing to realize that their partners were often participants in the political economy and had their own separate agendas. Perhaps that is why the solid wall of support that eventually challenged school segregation failed to materialize in the fight for open housing. African Americans were unable to demonstrate to the League of Women Voters or to Eugene Pulliam that segregated housing interfered with civic interests. Never did African Americans rely solely on an argument that segregation and discrimination were immoral evils. Rather, they consistently demonstrated the costs of discrimination and their preparedness to compete in the open market for housing, jobs, and economic advancement. The barriers to their participation were artificial, yet real, and they attacked the structures of inequality. Unfortunately, in this competition, their victory was limited and long delayed.

Postscript

In the four years between 1951 and 1955, when Crispus Attucks High School made another run for the state basketball championship, white Indianapolis residents were able to accept the Attucks basketball team as their best chance for victory at the state level. It would have been difficult to judge otherwise, since Attucks dominated city play in the intervening years. Given the limited advancement in pressing social arenas, however, it is evident that white residents were able to compartmentalize their feelings concerning African Americans. Whites saw no hypocrisy in cheering Attucks on as an Indianapolis team while at the same time denying African Americans full participation in civic affairs. In 1951, African American representatives had hoped to use Attucks's exploits as a wedge to improve race relations in the city. Four years later, there was little hope that sport would provide the full remedy African Americans sought. Rather than elevate African Americans to a social and political strata of equality, whites changed the cultural meaning of sport.

In 1955, led by Oscar Robertson, Flap's younger and immensely talented brother, Crispus Attucks won the first of two consecutive state basketball championships. By the time Oscar Robertson led the Tigers, Indianapolis residents no longer wondered whether the team represented them. Instead, they acted as did any other community whose team had reached the highest levels of the tournament. The team members were no longer interlopers intruding into a private party; rather, they were fellow Indianapolis citizens. In 1955, Attucks was not constrained with concerns about the civility of their play, for they played with seeming abandon. Coach Crowe had vowed that the next time they reached the finals his team would be ready. They were. However, so was Indianapolis—more ready than it had been in 1951. Suzanne Mitten-Owen, a white student at Shortridge at the time, recalled that the state championship that Attucks won in 1955 brought a "pride to the whole city, which I think helped break down a lot of the color barriers because those kids belonged to Indianapolis."[1] Mitton-Owen's comments reinforced the seeming racial and civic solidarity present at the title game. During the game against Gary Roosevelt, cheerleaders from the Indianapolis area high schools joined the Crispus Attucks cheer line.[2] Whites had resolved their ambivalent feelings about Attucks and its black players, and they had done so by compartmentalizing their feelings about blacks and their athletic prowess. Robertson noted how the climate had changed since his brother played on the team in 1951: "We became the team. The city team. It wasn't Crispus Attucks at the final game. It was Indianapolis Attucks. . . . Attucks being successful in basketball really gave people a lot better outlook on life. There was not much for blacks to look forward to except going to jobs with a dead end door."[3] By 1955, Attucks players and the city's African Americans no longer expected their play to translate into greater civic opportunities. Accordingly, they did not react when the victory parade that traditionally led to the downtown circle through the heart of the city instead ended up at Northwestern Park, a territory well known to Attucks's African American players. Bill Swatts, a member of Attucks's team, recalled that he was exactly where he wanted to be, with *his* people, in *his* neighborhood. "There was no place I would have rather been that night," he said, "no people I would have rather been with. I was just so happy."[4] For Oscar Robertson, the move to Northwestern Park was insulting and led him to take an early leave from the celebration for the solitude of his father's house. His answer to his father's concern and unasked question, and despite the white cheerleaders who had joined the Attucks cheer line, was a simple indictment: "Dad, they don't want us."[5] Their victory, as were many ensuing political victories, would be symbolic and of true value only to the African American community. The ambivalence represented in Swatts's and Robertson's feelings about the rerouted parade aptly captures the complication present in African American life and protest in Indianapolis. Their celebration of a significant achievement occurred in a manner and place separate from the larger community. For some, the celebration and achievement was enough to sustain and validate their presence. For others, like Oscar Robertson, repeated attempts to marginalize African Americans into proscribed areas and roles was a constant reminder of the inequalities present in many areas of daily life.

While blacks worked to open the "dead end" door, they took rest from their labors by cheering Attucks's basketball team. The team helped sustain African Americans in their fight to obtain full citizenship. The feeling in the African American community for Attucks's basketball team had never been ambivalent. Attucks continued to be a cultural haven for the black community. African Americans cheered and supported a group of young men who represented them in open competition with whites. African Americans from all over Indianapolis, whatever their neighborhood or their length of stay in the city, regardless of class or education, irrespective of occupation or station, rallied around the basketball team. In so doing, they reaffirmed that they were a constituency in the political economy, and a force in their own right.

NOTES

Introduction

1. Earline Rae Ferguson, "Blacks in Antebellum Indianapolis, 1820–1860," in *Indiana's African-American Heritage: Essays from Black History News & Notes* (Indianapolis: Indiana Historical Society, 1993), 123–124.

2. Randy Roberts, *"But They Can't Beat Us": Oscar Robertson and the Crispus Attucks Tigers* (Indianapolis: Indiana Historical Society, 1999), 3–4.

3. Kamau Jywanza, interview by the author, tape recording, January 10, 1994, Indianapolis, Indiana.

4. Thomas C. Holt, "Whither Now and Why?" in Darlene Clark Hine, *The State of Afro-American History: Past, Present, and Future* (Baton Rouge: Louisiana State University, 1989), 4.

5. During much of the first half of the twentieth century, Indianapolis had one of the largest proportions of African Americans in the northern states. Jon C. Teaford, *Cities of the Heartland: The Rise and Fall of the Industrial Midwest* (Lafayette, Ind.: Purdue University Press, 1993).

6. See Arnold R. Hirsch, *Making the Second Ghetto: Race and Housing in Chicago, 1940–1960* (Cambridge: Cambridge University Press, 1983); Kenneth L. Kusmer, *A Ghetto Takes Shape: Black Cleveland, 1870–1930* (Urbana: University of Illinois Press, 1976); Gilbert Osofsky, *Harlem: The Making of a Ghetto: Negro New York, 1890–1930* (New York: Harper & Row, 1963); Kimberley L. Phillips, *AlabamaNorth* (Urbana: University of Illinois Press, 1999); Allan H. Spear, *Black Chicago: The Making of a Negro Ghetto, 1890–1920* (Chicago: University of Chicago Press, 1967); Richard W. Thomas, *Life for Us Is What We Make It* (Bloomington: Indiana University Press, 1992); Joe William Trotter, *Black Milwaukee: The Making of an Industrial Proletariat, 1915–1945* (Urbana: University of Illinois Press, 1985).

7. Emma Lou Thornbrough, *Indiana Blacks in the Twentieth Century* (Bloomington: Indiana University Press, 2000), 49.

8. Ibid., 77.

9. Many scholars have commented on the contiguous pattern of African American housing development, but perhaps none as graphically as James R. Grossman's depiction of Chicago's "Black Belt." James R. Grossman, *Land of Hope: Chicago, Black Southerners, and the Great Migration* (Chicago: University of Chicago Press, 1989), 127.

10. Walter Maddux Collection, Manuscript 510, Box 2, Indiana Historical Society, Indianapolis, Indiana.

11. Record Group 31, Records of the Federal Housing Administration, Research and Statistics Division, Housing Market Date, 1938–52, Boxes 6 & 9, National Archives, College Park, Maryland. Robert Barrows demonstrated that Indianapolis residents were far less likely to relocate than were residents from nearby states. In fact, Indianapolis seemed a little out of step with its intrastate neighbors. South Bend had a persistence relocation rate of 29 percent during the latter decades of the nineteenth century, while Indianapolis had a persistence relocation rate of 69 percent. Robert G. Barrows, "A Demographic Analysis of Indianapolis, 1870–1920" (Ph.D. dissertation, Indiana University, 1977), 118–119.

12. Walter Maddux Collection, Manuscript 510, Box 2, Folder 9, Indiana Historical Society, Indianapolis, Indiana.

13. Kusmer, *A Ghetto Takes Shape,* 86–90.

14. With the exception of Unigov, many of the forces described above mimic those found in similarly sized cities in the lower Midwest. Where appropriate, I will refer the reader to material to compare Indianapolis's experience with that of other cities in the lower Midwest. Comparisons are always problematic because no two localities, regardless of how similarly situated, are the same. The task is further complicated because few historical studies have concentrated on the period after World War II. Earl Lewis and Thomas J. Sugrue are noteworthy examples of scholars who have extended urban analysis beyond the World War II period. Earl Lewis, *In Their Own Interests: Race, Class, and Power in Twentieth Century Norfolk, Virginia* (Berkeley: University of California Press, 1991); Thomas J. Sugrue, *The Origins of the Urban Crisis: Race and Inequality in Postwar Detroit* (Princeton, N. J.: Princeton University Press, 1996).

15. See Floyd B. Barbour, ed., *The Black Power Revolt* (Boston: Extending Horizons Books, 1968); Robert H. Brisbane, *Black Activism: Racial Revolution in the United States, 1954–1970* (Valley Forge, Pa.: Judson Press, 1974); James S. Hirsch, *Riot and Remembrance: The Tulsa Race War and Its Legacy* (Boston: Houghton Mifflin Co., 2002); Robin D. G. Kelley, *Hammer and Hoe: Alabama Communists during the Great Depression* (Chapel Hill: University of North Carolina Press, 1990); August Meier, John Bracey, Jr., and Elliott Rudwick, eds., *Black Protest in the Sixties* (New York: Markus Wiener Publishing, 1991); Arthur I. Waskow, *From Race Riot to Sit-In, 1919 and the 1960's: A Study in the Connections between Conflict and Violence* (Garden City, N.Y.: Doubleday & Company, 1966).

1. More than a Game

1. Scholars have frequently defined a community by hallmarks such as family, historic preservations, religious beliefs, neighborhoods, and social organizations. Recreational activities are equally important, although less frequently discussed. Within urban environments where, how, and with whom recreational activities occurred were not always determined by choice. Such was the case in Indianapolis, where a strict legal code created, among other things, segregated public parks, swimming pools, and theater seating. Where the law did not dictate it, racial and ethnic groups frequently segregated themselves at churches, nightclubs, and other public places such as basketball arenas. See Allan H. Spear, *Black Chicago: The Making of a Negro Ghetto, 1890–1920* (Chicago: University of Chicago Press, 1967); Gilbert Osofsky, *Harlem: The Making of a Ghetto* (New York: Harper & Row, 1963); Arnold R. Hirsch, *Making the Second Ghetto: Race and Housing in Chicago, 1940–1960* (Cambridge: Cambridge University Press, 1983).

2. Robin D. G. Kelley went even further in detailing the significance of leisure among African American workers in the South. For Kelley, the places blacks played—clubs and blues halls, parties, and dance rooms—were the places in which they recuperated from labor and found the strength to endure. It was in these "spaces of pleasure" that the solidarity later shown at political mass meetings formed. Ignoring complaints from religious leaders and the black middle class, African Americans packed nightspots on Friday and Saturday nights. Robin D. G. Kelley, "'We Are Not What We Seem': Rethinking Black Working Class Opposition in the Jim Crow South," *Journal of American History* 80, no. 1 (June 1993): 75–112.

3. Frederick Doyle Kershner, Jr., "A Social and Cultural History of Indianapolis, 1860–1914" (Ph.D. dissertation, University of Wisconsin, 1950), 84.

4. Quoted in Robert G. Barrows, "A Demographic Analysis of Indianapolis, 1870–1920" (Ph.D. dissertation, Indiana University, 1977), 42.

5. Ibid., 80–84.

6. Other cities with a smaller percentage of African American residents were able to elect alderman who represented their concerns, a tactic unavailable to Indianapolis's black community. Black Republicans in Chicago, for example, were able to exert considerable influence both because of their cohesiveness and because the white-dominated machine was willing to work with them for mutual benefit. Kenneth L. Kusmer, "The Black Urban Experience," in Hine, *The State of Afro-American History*, 119.

7. William A. Blomquist, "Government," in David J. Bodenhamer and Robert G. Barrows, eds., *The Encyclopedia of Indianapolis* (Bloomington: Indiana University Press, 1994), 86–93; Linda Weintraut, "The Limits of Enlightened Self-Interest: Business Power in Indianapolis, 1900–1977" (Ph.D. dissertation, Indiana University, 2001).

8. Mark D. Higbee, "W.E.B. DuBois, F.B. Ransom, the Madam Walker Company, and Black Business Leadership in the 1930s," *Indiana Magazine of History* LXXXIX (June 1993): 101–124; Gloria J. Gibson-Hudson, "To All Classes; to All Races; This House Is Dedicated: The Walker Theatre Revisited," in Wilma Gibbs, ed., *Indiana's African-American Heritage* (Indianapolis: Indiana Historical Society, 1993), 55.

9. In 1910, nearly 22,000 African Americans lived in Indianapolis and constituted 9.3 percent of the population, the highest percentage of any city north of the Ohio River. James J. Divita, "Demography and Ethnicity," in Bodenhamer and Barrows, eds., *The Encyclopedia of Indianapolis*, 55.

10. Monroe H. Little, Jr., "Civil Rights," in Bodenhamer and Barrows, eds., *The Encyclopedia of Indianapolis*, 439.

11. Emma Lou Thornbrough, "Segregation in Indiana during the Klan Era of the 1920's," *The Mississippi Valley Historical Review*, vol. 47, no. 4 (March 1961): 594–618.

12. For a discussion of the virtues society attributed to sport, see Gail Bederman, *Manliness and Civilization: A Cultural History of Race and Gender in the United States, 1880–1917* (Chicago: University of Chicago Press, 1995).

13. Quoted in Richard O. Davies, *America's Obsession: Sports and Society since 1945* (New York: Harcourt Brace & Company, 1994), 103.

14. The positive characteristics of participation in sports lessened as African American involvement grew. For a fuller discussion of the debate surrounding black college entry into intercollegiate sports see, Patrick B. Miller, "To 'Bring the Race along Rapidly': Sport, Student Culture, and Educational Mission at Historically Black Colleges during the Interwar Years," *History of Education Quarterly* 35, no. 2 (Summer 1995): 111–133. For a discussion on the varying definitions of manhood, see Bederman, *Manliness and Civilization*.

15. *Indianapolis Recorder*, August 6, 1927, January 1, 1949.

16. *Indianapolis Magazine*, May 1972, 33a. Although many Indianapolis blacks have memories similar to Howard Owens's, in 1949 an *Indianapolis News* article was headlined "Avenue Not Social Hub for Negroes." By this time, the lights on Indiana Avenue were beginning to dim. In the 1950s, it was still the "heart" of the community, but it was revered more for its past than its present. In their search for entertainment in a blacks-only environment, African Americans turned to a "myriad of private clubs, social orders, fraternities and sororities." In so doing, they recreated the class-conscious environment the Avenue had promised to alleviate. *Indianapolis News*, Nov. 18, 1949.

17. Lockefield Gardens was a 784-unit public housing complex solely inhabited by African

Americans. Developed in 1937 by the Housing Division of the Federal Emergency Administration of Public Works and the Advisory Committee on Housing of Indianapolis, Lockefield Gardens was in the center of Indianapolis's oldest black neighborhood and only a few blocks from Crispus Attucks High School. In its design and site plan, Lockefield Gardens was the model for public housing projects across the United States. Unlike many housing projects that followed, Lockefield Gardens was a community of more than simple residential structures; the plan included an elementary school, a play yard, and ample living space between and behind apartment buildings.

18. *Indianapolis Recorder,* March 17, 1951.

19. Scholars have noted recreation's importance in the creation of community—mostly in its impact on working-class popular culture. In his study of Worcester, Massachusetts, Roy Rosenzweig emphasized that knowledge of the leisure activities of the city's working class would enable scholars to understand more fully how workers viewed themselves and society. Workers fought to establish an eight-hour workday in order to leave time for socializing without the censure or permission of an overbearing middle class. Their victory in achieving their goal displayed conflicts in culture and class relationships, for when they played, they did so in the fashion in which they lived—racial and ethnic groups separated from each other, men separated from women, workers from people of means. See Gerald R. Gems, *Windy City Wars: Labor, Leisure, and Sport in the Making of Chicago* (Lanham, Md.: Scarecrow Press, 1997); John Hoberman, *Darwin's Athletes: How Sport Has Damaged Black America and Preserved the Myth of Race* (Boston: Houghton Mifflin, 1997). In his study of sandlot baseball in Pittsburgh, Rob Ruck probably best described the role sport played in African American communities, especially those beset with segregation. Rob Ruck, *Sandlot Seasons: Sport in Black Pittsburgh* (Urbana: University of Illinois Press, 1987); David Nassau, *Going Out: The Rise and Fall of Public Amusements* (New York: Basic Books, 1993); Roy Rosenzweig, *Eight Hours for What We Will* (Cambridge: Cambridge University Press, 1983); Kenneth L. Shropshire, *In Black and White: Race and Sports in America* (New York: New York University Press, 1996).

20. Ruck, *Sandlot Seasons,* 14.

21. In the official handbook of the organization, a notice to members read, "Do not compete with Indiana public High Schools that are non-members nor with public High Schools in other states that are not members of their state associations." Indiana High School Athletic Association, *Handbook and Report of the Board of Control,* 1928.

22. Constitution of Indiana High School Athletic Association. Article 2 (Membership), sections 1–3, 1904.

23. Ray Crowe, interview, "IUPUI: The Evolution of an Urban University," Indiana University–Purdue University at Indianapolis. Special Collections.

24. The Indiana High School Athletic Association, *Handbook and Report of the Board of Control,* 1942, 148.

25. Ray Crowe, interview. Perhaps the reception given to Attucks by rural teams is further evidence of the claim made by cultural critic Nelson George, who argues that the black aesthetic displayed in jazz music, individual virtuosity in an ensemble, was ably represented by basketball players who broke from the regimented, stationary style synonymous with 1950s-era basketball. Nelson George, *Elevating the Game* (New York: HarperCollins, 1992), 60–63.

26. Until recently, Indiana did not classify its high schools by enrollment. It was typical for the field to include over 750 schools in the single-elimination tournament. Davies, *America's Obsession,* 104–106.

27. *Indianapolis Star,* March 1, 1951, March 5, 1951.

28. David Stoelk, director, "Indy in the 50's" (produced by WFYI Television, Indianapolis, Indiana, 1995).

29. The Indiana tournament proceeded from sectionals, which usually included one or two counties, to regionals held at sixteen locations around the state. The third round, the semi-state, held at four locations, produced the final four teams that would compete at the state finals. Only the winners of each stage advanced to the next level. In the end, generally speaking, representatives from the northern, eastern, western, and southern part of the state reached the final round of the tournament.

30. The peculiar plan for desegregation in Indianapolis called for integration to occur one grade at a time beginning with kindergarten. Students would attend the high school where their elementary school directed them prior to the 1949 law. If the distance of that high school from the student's home was greater than two miles, then the school board would entertain appeals for a change.

31. *Indianapolis Star,* March 1, 1951.

32. *Indianapolis Star,* March 3, 1951. One disgruntled Indianapolis resident complained in a letter to the *Indianapolis News,* "Why, oh why can't we get something different on our radios these days? Nothing but 'sectionals' everywhere I turn the dial. For those who like basketball, fine—but everyone simply can't like the same things, and I know of several who are disgusted when they can't get anything else from so many stations. And after the sectionals, then other games are to be forced on us." *Indianapolis News,* March 5, 1951.

33. *Indianapolis News,* March 2, 1951, March 6, 1951.

34. *Indianapolis Star,* March 5, 1951.

35. Randy Roberts, "The Shot," *Traces* 9, no. 3 (Summer 1997): 7.

36. Flap Robertson was the older brother of National Basketball Association Hall of Fame player Oscar Robertson.

37. Roberts, "The Shot," 6–8; *Indianapolis Star,* March 5, 6, and 7, 1951; *Indianapolis Recorder,* March 10 and 17, 1951; Stoelk, "Indy in the 50's"; Crowe, interview.

38. *Indianapolis Star,* March 5, 1951.

39. *Indianapolis Recorder,* March 17, 1951.

40. *Indianapolis Star,* March 12, 1951.

41. Roberts, "The Shot," 11.

42. *Indianapolis Recorder,* March 17, 1951.

43. Ibid.

44. Ibid.

45. Roberts, "The Shot," 11–13.

46. Richard B. Pierce, "Beneath the Surface: African-American Community Life in Indianapolis, 1945–1970" (Ph.D. dissertation, Indiana University, 1996), 29.

47. Ibid., 67–73.

48. Ibid., 106–112.

49. To an outsider it may have appeared that Indianapolis's black residents were complacent in their acceptance of unequal and discriminatory treatment. Beneath the surface, however, a fierce battle was taking place over the structure and culture of the city. The battle was especially difficult for an outsider to notice because it took place in meeting rooms, at the statehouse, and in the courts. It was not a conflict that transpired on the streets or was shouted through a bullhorn. African American resistance was conducted under rules long established by Indianapolis citizens. Both black and white newspapers in the 1950s and 1960s were concerned with the potential violence social inequities could spawn. Many editorialists agreed that it was communication between the races that prevented violence from erupting in Indianapolis. Pierce, 29

50. William H. Chafe, *Civilities and Civil Rights: Greensboro, North Carolina, and the Black Struggle for Freedom* (New York: Oxford University Press, 1980), 6–9.

51. Kevin Gaines, *Uplifting the Race: Black Leadership, Politics, and Culture in the Twentieth Century* (Chapel Hill: University of North Carolina Press, 1996), 16.

52. George, *Elevating the Game,* 119–120.

53. Found in David Remnick, *King of the World* (New York: Vintage Press, 1998), 18–22. Quote is found on page 22.

54. Starling James settled in Indianapolis in 1927, ironically just as the city was about to institute segregated secondary education. He began his organizing efforts soon after settling in by forming the While-Away Bridge Club. Struck by the number of black social clubs in the city, James called together the leaders of nine of these clubs in 1937 and the Federation of Associated Clubs (FAC) was born.

James created the FAC in the face of strong opposition from certain segments of the black community. Black social clubs were under attack as worthless and as promoting class distinctions, but James and the members of the FAC considered themselves promoters of middle-class values. James wanted to educate the black community to uphold similar values and he subsequently published a series of articles entitled "Guide Right," to help popularize and define his views. James was hardly a cultural radical and in fact admonished blacks for "detrimental" behavior that reflected unfavorably upon the entire black community. In James's view, blacks were at least partly responsible for their circumstance: "We are not as polite and courteous to others as we should be. Manners are one of the prerequisites of an outstanding personality. Also, some of us are rather crude and loud. We must cultivate softness in our voice." James wanted to show that clubs could do something for the larger community.

The FAC was one of the most successful organizations in the city. James was able to demonstrate that social clubs did not have to be self-serving. Within ten years of incorporation, the number of groups belonging to the FAC had grown to 125. FAC's stated purpose was to promote social, civic, and economic benefits for the black community. Throughout his long tenure as president (1937–1969), James kept FAC intimately involved with some of the more pressing political issues in the post–World War II period. In many ways, the FAC was the most progressive large group in Indianapolis. Pierce, 50–52.

55. Mrs. Rosa Tolliver, mother of Attucks guard Joe Tolliver, was not among the crowd. Her family would not allow her to watch from the stands because she had almost passed out during the Anderson game. *Indianapolis Recorder,* March 24, 1951.

56. Roberts, "The Shot," 13.

57. Bob Williams, *Hoosier Hysteria! Indiana High School Basketball* (South Bend, Ind.: Hardwood Press, 1997), 42.

58. *Indianapolis Recorder,* March 24, 1951.

59. Ibid.

60. Ibid., March 31, 1951.

61. Ibid.

62. *Indianapolis News,* March 20, 1951.

2. "We Have Given You No Extremists"

1. Eric R. Jackson, "The Endless Journey: The Black Struggle for Quality Public Schools in Indianapolis, Indiana, 1900–1949" (Ed.D. dissertation, University of Cincinnati, 2000), 41.

2. Indianapolis Public Schools, *Annual Report* (Indianapolis, 1866) 16–17.

3. Quote found in Emma Lou Thornbrough, *The Negro in Indiana before 1900. A Study of a Minority* (Indianapolis: Indiana Historical Society, 1957), 318.

4. Jackson, "The Endless Journey," 18–24.

5. Indiana *House Journal,* 1896, 489, 746, 751–754; Emma Lou Thornbrough, *The Indianapolis Story: School Segregation and Desegregation in a Northern City,* typescript (Indianapolis: Indiana Historical Society, 1992), 12.

6. Thornbrough, *The Negro in Indiana before 1900,* 337–338; Thornbrough, *The Indianapolis Story,* 30; *Indianapolis Freeman,* January 23, 1897, February 20, 1897; *Indianapolis World,* January 9, 1897, January 30, 1897.

7. *Indiana Daily News,* September 2, 1921, November 9, 1921.

8. Emma Lou Thornbrough, *The Indianapolis Story,* 28, 59.

9. Quoted in School Commissioner Minutes, *Book X* (Indianapolis, 1922) 30, 396–397.

10. James H. Madison, *Indiana through Tradition and Change* (Indianapolis: Indiana Historical Society, 1982), 12.

11. *Indianapolis News,* December 9, 1922, December 13, 1922; School Commissioner Minutes, *Book X,* 63; *Indianapolis Freeman,* March 1, 1924.

12. Thornbrough, *The Indianapolis Story,* 38.

13. The Klan has often borne the brunt of the blame for segregated schools in Indianapolis. The Citizens Council used as its campaign rhetoric for the next thirty years a variation of the theme, "We got the Klan out of the schools." Citizens Council candidates defeated Klan-supported members, but once in position did little to slow the transition to segregated schools. For the next forty years, under the able leadership of Judge John L. Niblack, the Citizens Council controlled the selection of school board members. Until 1964, a Citizens Council nominee held every seat on the school board. During its reign, construction of new schools, implementation of a separate race-based school system, and an intense legal fight in defense of segregation continued unabated under the auspices of a school board that had ever-changing membership but a consistent philosophy of race-based student placement. Thornbrough, *The Indianapolis Story,* 59; James H. Madison, *The Indiana Way: A State History* (Bloomington: Indiana University Press, 1990), 294.

14. Ibid., 40.

15. *Indianapolis Freeman,* March 1, 1924; Emma Lou Thornbrough, "Segregation in Indiana during the Klan Era of the 1920's," *The Mississippi Valley Historical Review,* vol. 47, no. 4 (March 1961): 598. See chapter 3.

16. *Indianapolis Recorder,* August 6, 1927, January 1, 1949.

17. Joseph Taylor, interview by the author, tape recording, Indianapolis, Ind., March 5, 1994.

18. Willard Ransom, interview, Indiana University Center for the Study of History and Memory, Bloomington, Indiana; Thornbrough, *The Indianapolis Story,* 43.

19. David Stoelk, director, "Indy in the 50's" (produced by WFYI Television, Indianapolis, Indiana, 1995).

20. *Indianapolis Recorder,* September 17, 1938.

21. *Indianapolis Recorder,* January 26, 1946; Emma Lou Thornbrough, *Indiana Blacks in the Twentieth Century,* ed. Lana Ruegamer (Bloomington and Indianapolis: Indiana University Press, 2000), 144.

22. Indianapolis School Commissioners Minutes, *Book OO* (Indianapolis, 1946) 1517, 1524.

23. School Commissioner Minutes, *Book OO,* 1537–1538; *Indianapolis Recorder,* February 16, 1946; September 7, 1946. Gary, the Indiana city with the second largest African American population, had already integrated its schools.

24. Fay Williams, interview by the author, tape recording, Indianapolis, Ind., February 14, 1994.

25. *Indianapolis Recorder,* December 14, 1946; School Commissioners Minutes, *Book OO,* 1740–1742.

26. School Commissioners Minutes, *Book OO,* 1740–1742; *Indianapolis Times,* December 31, 1946.

27. Indiana *Senate Journal,* 1947, 77, 132; Indiana *House Journal,* 1947, 410; *Indiana Laws,* 1947, 157–160.

28. Indiana *House Journal* (1947), 151, 302–303; *Indianapolis Star,* January 30, 1947.

29. Quoted in Thornbrough, *The Indianapolis Story,* 96–98.

30. *Indianapolis Star,* February 21, 1947; *Indianapolis Times,* February 21, 1947; Statement of Indianapolis Board of Commissioners, February 20, 1947, NAACP Papers.

31. Thornbrough, *The Indianapolis Story,* 132–135; "Official Report of the 1951 Study on Racial Attitudes of the Protestant Churches of Indianapolis and Marion County," Located in card catalogue under Indiana-Negroes-Indianapolis, Indiana State Library, Indianapolis, Indiana.

32. Thornbrough, *The Indianapolis Story,* 96–100; *Indianapolis Star,* February 21, 1947; *Indianapolis Times,* February 21, 1947; *Indianapolis Recorder,* March 1, 1947; Indiana *House Journal,* 1947, 672–673.

33. Madison, *The Indiana Way,* 310.

34. Roselyn Richardson described her increasing anger over the segregated school system in this way: "And I was getting madder and madder the more I thought about it before my child got to be of school age, that we got to pass three white schools including one that's four blocks from home, to get to a black school. Then when I went over and looked at the black school I got madder. Because it was so crowded, they had classes in the hall. And I don't know, I said my child isn't going to do this." Roselyn Richardson, interview by the author, tape recording, Indianapolis, Ind., February 24, 1994.

35. The Institute brought speakers such as Eleanor Roosevelt and Ralph Bunche to speak on how important it was for young people to work for peace. Roselyn Richardson was a field secretary for the Green Service Committee, and in that role recruited college students to spread the committee's message. She alleged the program was a precursor to John Kennedy's VISTA program, which used Green Service materials. Richardson, interview.

36. *Indianapolis News,* November 15, 1949, November 17, 1949.

37. *Indianapolis Times,* July 16, 1947; Thornbrough, *The Indianapolis Story,* 102–104.

38. *Indianapolis Times,* July 16, 1947.

39. Ibid., October 12, 1947.

40. Group II, NAACP 1940–1955, Box C-55, October, 1947, NAACP Papers.

41. School Commissioners Minutes, *Book PP* (1947), 1917. Eventually, by the late 1950s, after neighborhood demographics began to stabilize, the board's rallying cry would become "neighborhood schools" are best for the student and community.

42. Andrew Brown, interview by the author, tape recording, Indianapolis, Ind., March 10, 1992; Williams, interview; Willard Ransom, interview by the author, tape recording, Indianapolis, Ind., March 12, 1994; David J. Bodenhamer and Robert G. Barrows, eds., *The Encyclopedia of Indianapolis* (Bloomington: Indiana University Press, 1994), 5–14; *Indianapolis Times,* August 2, 1959.

43. Quoted in Thornbrough, *The Indianapolis Story,* 106–107.

44. Ibid., 107–108.

45. Quoted in ibid., 108.

46. Gloster Current to William T. Ray, February 17, 1948, NAACP Papers; Ransom, interview.

47. Dr. Max Wolff, "Pilot Study as to the Kind of Survey Best Suited to Indianapolis' Needs, Re: Segregation of School System," June 23, 1948, NAACP Papers.

48. The *Indianapolis Recorder* named Eugene Pulliam to its Race Relations Honor Roll in 1948 largely in response to his editorials condemning segregated schools. It was a singular honor. *Indianapolis Recorder*, January 1, 1949.

49. Henry J. Richardson to Thurgood Marshall, October 23, 1948, NAACP Papers.

50. *Indianapolis Recorder*, June 15, 1948; Thornbrough, *The Indianapolis Story*, 112–117; Henry J. Richardson to Thurgood Marshall, October 23, 1948, NAACP Papers.

51. Richardson, interview.

52. *Indianapolis Times*, February 23, 1949, February 24, 1949; *Indianapolis Star*, February 23, 1949, February 24, 1949; *Indianapolis Recorder*, March 19, 1949.

53. Thornbrough, *The Indianapolis Story*, 120–121; Indiana *House Journal*, 1949, 711–712; *Indianapolis Star*, March 1, 1949.

54. Thornbrough, *The Indianapolis Story*, 122–123; Ransom, interview; Indiana *Senate Journal*, 1949, 814.

55. *Indianapolis Recorder*, March 5, 1949.

56. *Indianapolis Recorder*, March 12, 1949; Press Release, March 17, 1949, NAACP Papers.

57. Thornbrough, *The Indianapolis Story*, 126–127. Future school boards would prove especially adept in gerrymandering school districts to maintain racial exclusiveness when a neighborhoods racial composition changed. Judge S. Hugh Dillin found that "according to the evidence, there have been approximately 350 boundary changes in the system [IPS] since 1954. More than 90% of these promoted segregation." Quoted in William E. Marsh, "The Indianapolis Experience: The Anatomy of a Desegregation Case," *Indiana Law Review* 9 (1976): 900.

58. School Commissioners Minutes, *Book QQ*, (Indianapolis, 1949), 169; Thornbrough, *The Indianapolis Story*, 126–129; *Indianapolis Recorder*, April 16, 1949.

59. Quoted in Thornbrough, *The Indianapolis Story*, 136; *Indianapolis Times*, October 10, 1954; *Indianapolis News*, November 30, 1953; Thornbrough, *The Indianapolis Story*, 129.

60. *Indianapolis News*, November 25, 1953, November 26, 1953.

61. Marsh, "Indianapolis Experience," 901.

62. Thornbrough, *The Indianapolis Story*, 150; *Indianapolis Times*, May 22, 1959.

63. *Indianapolis Times*, May 22, 1959.

64. *Indianapolis Recorder*, June 27, 1959; *Indianapolis Star*, October 27, 1959; Thornbrough, *The Indianapolis Story*, 152.

65. *Indianapolis News*, June 21, 1959, June 30, 1959; *Indianapolis Recorder*, July 4, 1959; Thornbrough, *The Indianapolis Story*, 151–152.

66. School Commissioners Minutes, *Book AAA* (Indianapolis, 1959), 880–881; *Indianapolis Recorder*, July 11, 1959, July 18, 1959; *Indianapolis Times*, October 25, 1959.

67. *Indianapolis Recorder*, October 31, 1959.

68. Thornbrough, *The Indianapolis Story*, 158–160; *Indianapolis Times*, October 1, 1959, October 23, 1959.

69. *Indianapolis News*, October 29, 1959, October 30, 1959; *Indianapolis Star*, October 31, 1959, November 1, 1959.

70. *Indianapolis Star*, November 4, 1959.

71. *Indianapolis Recorder*, December 1, 1962, May 18, 1963, October 5, 1963; Thornbrough, *The Indianapolis Story*, 163–165; Earl Lewis, *In Their Own Interests: Race, Class, and Power in Twentieth Century Norfolk, Virginia* (Berkeley: University of California Press, 1991).

72. Thornbrough, *Indiana Blacks in the Twentieth Century*, 154.

73. *Indianapolis Recorder*, December 28, 1963.

74. Stephen Pollack to Mark Gray, April 23, 1968, in School Commissioners Minutes, *Book III* (Indianapolis, 1968), 2053–2065.

75. Thornbrough, *Indiana Blacks in the Twentieth Century*, 155.

76. Shortridge High School was the only deviation from the norm. Shortridge had long been regarded as the premiere high school in Indianapolis. Students interested in pursuing post-secondary education enrolled at Shortridge, regardless of where they lived in the city. With passage of the 1949 law and the spread of black neighborhoods directly south and west of Shortridge's 34th and Meridian location, it became increasingly difficult to preserve Short-ridge's all-white composition. In 1964, school board officials were able to circumvent the impending reality by labeling Shortridge a college prep school. Thornbrough, *The Indi-anapolis Story*, 213; Thornbrough, *Indiana Blacks in the Twentieth Century*, 156.

77. *Indianapolis Star*, April 22, 1969, May 1, 1969; *Indianapolis News*, May 12, 1969, De-cember 29, 1969; Thornbrough, *The Indianapolis Story*, 244.

78. Various organizations endorsed HEW's recommendation. Among them were the League of Women Voters, National Council of Jewish Women, YWCA, Community Action Against Poverty, and Southern Christian Leadership Conference. Thornbrough, *The Indi-anapolis Story*, 248–250.

79. *Indianapolis Recorder*, July 13, 1963; *Indianapolis News*, July 15, 1969.

80. Marsh, "Indianapolis Experience," 904–905.

81. Ibid., 952–954.

82. Ibid., 955–976, 986–992.

3. "We Were Always Fighting the Housing Battle"

1. Walter Maddux Collection, Manuscript 510, Box 2, Indiana Historical Society, In-dianapolis, Indiana.

2. White migrants from Appalachia also endured discriminatory housing practices. For more information on the challenges facing southern white migration to Indianapolis, see Chad Berry, "Social Highways: Southern White Migration to the Midwest, 1910–1990" (Ph.D. dissertation, Indiana University, 1995).

3. Many historians have written of the northern African American housing patterns. Allan Spear's examination of Chicago is illustrative. By 1915, African Americans primarily resided in south Chicago with easy access to jobs at railroad yards nearby and a reasonable distance to downtown. African Americans moved from ward to contiguous ward, with whites often moving away from areas whose racial composition was changing. Chicago's example was replicated in other northern urban communities, and the term "white flight" became a common expression in the American vernacular. African American urban pioneers often moved into neighborhoods where they paid far too much for the accommodations they re-ceived and where their new neighbors did not welcome them. The violence Arnold Hirsch detailed in Chicago as African Americans moved into white, working-class neighborhoods was not repeated to the same degree in Indianapolis. See Allan H. Spear, *Black Chicago: The Making of a Negro Ghetto, 1890–1920* (Chicago: University of Chicago Press, 1967), 11–14; Gilbert Osofsky, *Harlem: The Making of a Ghetto* (New York: Harper & Row, 1963), 17–35; Arnold R. Hirsch, *Making the Second Ghetto: Race and Housing in Chicago, 1940–1960* (Cam-bridge: Cambridge University Press, 1983), 68–76, 171–200.

4. Milwaukee's example may be most representative. Joe W. Trotter argues that Mil-

waukee's relatively small African American population became more ghettoized as proletarianization, the process of moving from domestic and personal service occupations to working-class labor jobs, became more prevalent. As Milwaukee's black population grew and successfully entered the working class, they became increasingly entrenched in the second and sixth wards. In 1910, African Americans almost exclusively inhabited one area spanning the second and sixth wards, covering thirty-five blocks. Joe William Trotter, *Black Milwaukee: The Making of an Industrial Proletariat, 1915–1945* (Urbana: University of Illinois Press, 1985), 65–68; see also John McGreevy, *Parish Boundaries: The Catholic Encounter with Race in the Twentieth-Century Urban America* (Chicago: University of Chicago Press, 1996).

5. James Divita, "Overview: Demography and Ethnicity," in David J. Bodenhamer and Robert G. Barrows, eds., *The Encyclopedia of Indianapolis* (Bloomington and Indianapolis: Indiana University Press, 1994), 55. At the time, New York City's population was 1.9 percent black, Chicago 2 percent, and Detroit 1.2 percent. Indianapolis's immigrant population, numbering 20,000, or 8.5 percent of the total, was low in comparison to other northern urban areas—New York 40.4 percent, Chicago 35.7 percent, and Detroit 33.6 percent.

6. Divita, "Overview: Demography and Ethnicity," 55–56; Robert G. Barrows, "A Demographic Analysis of Indianapolis: 1870–1920" (Ph.D. dissertation, Indiana University, 1977), 120–124. By the second decade of the twentieth century every ward contained some black residents and in only one-third of the city wards did African Americans constitute less than 5 percent of the total ward population.

7. Emma Lou Thornbrough, "African-Americans," in Bodenhamer and Barrows, *The Encyclopedia of Indianapolis*, 7.

8. *Indianapolis Freeman,* April 22, 1916.

9. *Indianapolis Freeman,* August 12, 1916.

10. For a good explanation of the division between public and private domains, see Earl Lewis, *In Their Own Interests: Race, Class, and Power in Twentieth Century Norfolk, Virginia* (Berkeley: University of California Press, 1991).

11. Emma Lou Thornbrough, "Segregation in Indiana during the Klan Era of the 1920's," *The Mississippi Valley Historical Review,* vol. 47, no. 4 (March 1961): 598; *Indianapolis Freeman,* March 1, 1924.

12. Record Group 31, Records of the Federal Housing Administration, Research and Statistics Division, Housing Market Date, 1938–52, Boxes 6 & 9, National Archives, College Park, Maryland. Robert Barrows demonstrated that Indianapolis residents were far less likely to relocate than were residents from nearby states. In fact, Indianapolis seemed a little out of step with its intrastate neighbors. South Bend had a persistence rate of 29 percent during the latter decades of the nineteenth century, while Indianapolis had a persistence rate of 69 percent. Barrows, "A Demographic Analysis of Indianapolis," 118–119.

13. Barrows, "A Demographic Analysis of Indianapolis," 119–134; Thornbrough, "African-Americans," 6.

14. Record Group 195, Records of the Federal Home Loan Bank Board, Home Owners Loan Corporation, Box 113, National Archives.

15. Record Group 195, Records of the Federal Home Loan Bank Board, Home Owners Loan Corporation, Box 114. National Archives. Quote is found on page 18.

16. Spear, *Black Chicago,* 12; Thornbrough, "African Americans," 7.

17. *Buchanan* v. *Warley,* 245 U.S. 60 (1917).

18. Barrows, "A Demographic Analysis of Indianapolis," 171–180; Thornbrough, "African-Americans," 7–8.

19. Flanner House Program Institute, October 6, 1939, Indianapolis, Indiana, Negroes—Indianapolis Collection, Indiana State Library.

20. *Indianapolis Star,* July 15, 1937.

21. Flanner House, *A Study of 454 Negro Households* (Flanner House, Indianapolis, Indiana, 1946).

22. Eugenia J. Hollis, "A Critical Analysis of Seventeen Studies of Housing Conducted in Indianapolis from 1935 to 1946" (Ph.D. dissertation, Indiana University, 1947), 42.

23. *Indianapolis Star,* March 2, 1952, March 5, 1952; *Indianapolis Times,* March 4, 1952.

24. *Indianapolis Star,* February 6, 1938, September 7, 1939; *Indianapolis Times,* January 23, 1957. In 1951 the Indianapolis Public Housing Authority charged the Indianapolis Real Estate Board with "sabotaging" public housing initiatives. *Indianapolis News,* November 28, 1951; *Indianapolis Star,* November 29, 1951.

25. Quote found in Roger William Riis and Webb Waldron, "Fortunate City," *Survey Graphic,* August 1945, 340; Hollis, "A Critical Analysis of Seventeen Studies of Housing Conducted in Indianapolis from 1935 to 1946," 5–22; Flanner House, *Flanner House and the Negro Community* (Indianapolis: Flanner House, 1939). Flanner House studied 1,501 families out of a total black population of 51,142. They examined physical conditions, degree of overcrowding, type of lighting, toilet facilities, heating facilities, and water supply. The study presents a reliable picture of the kind of housing occupied by African Americans. The WPA reported that 23,000 families were living in substandard dwelling units. Their study found that out of the 110,003 residential units on which detailed information was obtained, 15,323, or 14 percent, needed major repair or were unfit for use. Of these, 13,331 units, or 86 percent, were tenant-occupied. Fourteen percent of the population was living in physically substandard housing, and a large majority of these families were tenants. Real Property and Low Income Housing Surveys, Volume 1 (WPA, 1939), 42. The United States Bureau of the Census published figures which showed an even greater proportion of substandard housing than in the WPA report. In the 1940 census, 104,928 of the 116,598 dwelling units in Indianapolis were reported on in detail, and 18,523 of the reported units, or 17.6 percent, were classified as "needing major repair." United States Bureau of the Census, *Population and Housing Statistics for Census Tracts: 1940,* 3.

26. Hollis, "A Critical Analysis of Seventeen Studies of Housing Conducted in Indianapolis from 1935 to 1946"; See also Flanner House, *A Study of 454 Negro Households in the Redevelopment Area.*

27. Lisa E. McGuire, "Public Housing in Indianapolis," in History of Indianapolis Public Housing. Located at the Indianapolis Housing Authority, Indianapolis, Indiana. Whites, too, were eager to obtain public housing to replace the dilapidated housing that many faced. One project, titled Project H-1602 by the Public Works Administration, was shelved when President Franklin Roosevelt pulled the funding from the project. Record Group 196, Public Housing Administration, Box 122. National Archives.

28. Susan White, "The Avenue . . . Where the Black Man Has Always Been King," *Indianapolis Magazine,* May 1972, 33.

29. Preliminary Case Report Lockefield Gardens, Indianapolis, Indiana, n.d., Lockefield Gardens Collection, Indiana State Library.

30. *Indianapolis News,* September 7, 1970.

31. Fay Williams, interview by the author, tape recording, Indianapolis, Ind., February 14, 1994; Willard Ransom, interview, Indiana University Center for the Study of History and Memory, Bloomington, Indiana; Joseph Taylor, interview by the author, tape recording, Indianapolis, Ind., March 5, 1994.

32. The Health and Welfare Council of Indianapolis and Marion County, "A Report on Lockefield Garden Apartments and Negro Low-Rent Housing in Indianapolis," January 22, 1957 (Indianapolis: Indiana State Library).

33. *Indianapolis News,* April 30, 1937; Indianapolis *Star,* January 24, 1937, September 2, 1937.

34. Emma Lou Thornbrough, *Since Emancipation: A Short History of Indiana Negroes, 1863–1963* (n.p.: Indiana Division, American Negro Emancipation Centennial Authority, 1964), 81; Fay H. Williams, interview; Andrew J. Brown interview, interview by the author, tape recording, Indianapolis, Ind., March 10, 1992.

35. By 1959, the Army Finance Center at Fort Benjamin Harrison had about 1,700 African Americans in civil service jobs at an annual payroll of $7 million. *Indianapolis Times,* August 2, 1959.

36. Robert G. Barrows, "Silver Buckle on the Rust Belt," in Richard M. Bernard, ed., *Snowbelt Cities: Metropolitan Politics in the Northeast and Midwest since World War II* (Bloomington: Indiana University Press, 1990), 140.

37. *Journal of the Proceedings of the Common Council of the City of Indianapolis,* 1952, 17–18. The Housing Authority was created in March 1951 with the authority to examine spots for renewal. With this legislation, the council put all the housing authority's actions under their complete control. McGuire, 3.

38. The United States Housing Authority (USHA) was directed to funnel money to municipalities by lending up to 90 percent of the capital costs of a project to local officials. The USHA also subsidized construction and maintenance costs. However, the USHA only provided funding to duly constituted local housing agencies. Kenneth Jackson, *Crabgrass Frontier: The Suburbanization of the United States* (New York: Oxford University Press, 1985), 224.

39. Riis and Waldron, "Fortunate City," 339.

40. Clarence Wood, interview, November 28, 1995, Indiana University Center for the Study of History and Memory, Bloomington, Indiana.

41. Madison S. Jones to F. D. Coker, Chairman, Housing Committee Indiana Conference of NAACP, November 14, 1956, Group III, Box A-159, NAACP Papers.

42. Lockefield Garden Apartments Brochure, Record Group 196, Public Housing Administration, Box 122, National Archives.

43. William Taylor, interview by the author, tape recording, Bloomington, Ind., February 14, 1996; Mary Brookins, interview, December 5, 1995, Indiana University Center for the Study of History and Memory, Bloomington, Indiana.

44. The cost of the homes changed over time in relation to the rising cost of building materials.

45. Flanner House, *Flanner House and the Negro Community.*

46. Clarence Wood, interview, November 28, 1995, Indiana University Center for the Study of History and Memory, Bloomington, Indiana.

47. Henry J. Richardson to Cleo Blackburn, July 13, 1964, Richardson Collection; Rachael L. Drenovsky, "The Issue Now Is Open Occupancy: The Struggle for Fair Housing in Indianapolis, 1890–1968" (M.A. thesis, Indiana University, 2001), 73–74.

48. National Archives, Record Group 31, Records of the Federal Housing Administration, Box 6.

49. In the 1960s several African American professionals and business people built new suburban homes in the vicinity of Kessler Boulevard and Grandview Avenue, financed by a Louisville insurance company when local institutions rejected their applications. Bodenhamer and Barrows, *Encyclopedia of Indianapolis,* 138.

50. *Indianapolis News,* September 10, 1963.

51. Senior Lawyers Project Collection, M0574 (Willard Ransom, BV 2620; CT555-567), third interview, p. 10, Indiana Historical Society, Indianapolis, Indiana.

52. As opposition arose, Barton's support became more equivocal. Barton promised to

veto any legislation that the city legal department deemed unconstitutional, and he vowed to remain silent concerning the proposed legislation until it reached his desk. *Indianapolis Star,* February 20, 1964.

53. *Indianapolis News,* May 15, 1964.

54. *Indianapolis Times,* May 24, 1964.

55. *Indianapolis Star,* May 27, 1964.

56. *Indianapolis News,* February 10, 1965, November 21, 1963.

57. *Indianapolis Star,* June 10, 1964.

58. *Indianapolis Star,* December 11, 1966.

59. *Indianapolis Star,* July 7, 1964; *Indianapolis Times,* July 9, 1964.

60. *Indianapolis News,* December 20, 1967.

61. Interestingly, the first news article about BTNA referred to it as a "new interracial group whose purpose was to improve and maintain the neighborhood between 38th and 52nd and Route 421 and Illinois." *Indianapolis Star,* June 17, 1958. Quoted in Juliet Saltman, *A Fragile Movement: The Struggle for Neighborhood Stabilization* (New York: Greenwood Press, 1990), 39. Similar cooperative integrationist efforts took place in other suburban neighborhoods. Of particular note are the Highland-Kessler Civic League, the Devington Communities Association, and the Spring Mill Hoover Association for Residential Participation. Bodenhamer and Barrows, *Encyclopedia of Indianapolis,* 138.

62. Saltman, *A Fragile Movement,* 36–38, 70–74.

63. *Indianapolis Star,* June 17, 1958, in Saltman, *A Fragile Movement,* 38.

64. Saltman, *A Fragile Movement,* 50, 65–72.

65. Quoted in ibid., 48.

66. Ibid.

67. Ibid.

68. For a discussion of similar processes executed in other cities, see Ronald Bayor, "Roads to Racial Segregation: Atlanta in the Twentieth Century," *Journal of Urban History* 15 (1988): 3–21; Raymond A. Mohl, "Race and Space in the Modern City: Interstate-95 and the Black Community in Miami," in *Urban Policy in Twentieth-Century America* (New Brunswick, N.J.: Rutgers University Press, 1993), 100–158; and Thomas J. Sugrue, *The Origins of the Urban Crisis: Race and Inequality in Postwar Detroit* (Princeton, N.J.: Princeton University Press, 1996), 47–51.

69. Barrows, "Silver Buckle on the Rust Belt," 140–141.

70. John Walls, interview, "IUPUI: The Evolution of an Urban University," Ruth Lilly Special Collection and Archives, IUPUI Libraries, Indianapolis, Indiana.

71. *Indianapolis News,* November 21, 1966; *Indianapolis Star,* November 30, 1966.

72. Dr. Joseph Taylor, interview, "IUPUI: The Evolution of an Urban University Collection," IUPUI Special Collections.

73. Ida Edelin, interview by the author, tape recording, Indianapolis, Ind., December 5, 1995.

74. Walls, interview.

75. Charles Hardy, interview, "IUPUI: The Evolution of an Urban University, Interview dates: October 16, October 27, 1989 and January 3, 1990, IUPUI Special Collections, Indianapolis, Indiana, 11–14.

76. Maynard K. Hine, Indiana University Chancellor, to All IUPUI Students, October, 1971, Indiana University–Purdue University at Indianapolis folder, Indiana University Archives, Bloomington, Indiana.

77. Hardy, interview, 14. Hardy's impression of Torian may be colored by the con-

frontation the two men had. Hardy alleged that Torian threatened to kill him because of Hardy's participation in the purchase of neighborhood homes, 45.

78. John Liell, interview, "IUPUI: The Evolution of an Urban University," IUPUI Special Collections.

79. *Indianapolis News,* March 6, 1935; *Indianapolis Star,* February 16, 1940.

80. *Indianapolis Times,* December 3, 1941.

81. Ibid.; *The Negro in Indianapolis* (Cedar Rapids, Iowa: Magid and Associates, 1969).

82. Metropolitan Indianapolis Housing Study. Summary Report. IUPUI Library Special Collections, 2.

83. Ibid., 5.

84. Ibid., 32.

4. "You're Tired, Chile"

1. One of Hardrick's daughters believed the painter was depicting the type of life a high school student could expect without a proper education. Conversation with William E. Taylor, lecturer, African American Visual Art History, Indiana University–Purdue University Indianapolis, May 25, 1996.

2. Kevin Gaines, *Uplifting the Race: Black Leadership, Politics, and Culture in the Twentieth Century* (Chapel Hill: University of North Carolina Press, 1996), 1–17.

3. Walter Maddux Collection, Manuscript 510, Box 2, Folder 9, Indiana Historical Society.

4. United States Census Bureau, *1940 Population,* vol. 3, pt. 2, 985. Blacks outnumbered whites in three categories: janitors, servants (except private family), and communication and utility laborers.

5. Allan H. Spear, *Black Chicago: The Making of a Negro Ghetto, 1890–1920* (Chicago: University of Chicago Press, 1967), 29–41; Joe William Trotter, *Black Milwaukee: The Making of an Industrial Proletariat, 1915–1945* (Urbana: University of Illinois Press, 1985), 13–18.

6. Booth Tarkington, *The Magnificent Ambersons* (Garden City, N.Y.: Doubleday Page, 1918).

7. Flanner House Program Institute, October 6, 1939 (Located under Indiana-Negroes-Indianapolis), Indiana State Library, Indianapolis.

8. Dallas Daniels, "History of the Federated Association of Clubs 1939–1949" (M.A. thesis, Butler University, 1975), 11–16.

9. Flanner House History Collection, Flanner House Library, Indianapolis, Indiana; Fay Williams, interview by the author, tape recording, Indianapolis, Ind., February 14, 1994.

10. Parris Guichard and Lester Brown, *Blacks in the City: A History of the National Urban League* (Boston: Little, Brown and Company, 1971).

11. Williams, interview. Few incidents demonstrated Flanner House's commitment to avoidance of direct, confrontational action more than the firing of Wilson Head. Head, president of the Interracial Civil Rights Committee and executive director of the Indianapolis NAACP, lost his job as a social worker at Flanner House when the NAACP fought to get downtown restaurants to extend their service to African Americans. *Shreveport Sun,* January 10, 1948. Found in Indianapolis Branch news, NAACP Papers.

12. The Quaker's American Friends Service Committee founded the Association for Merit Employment in 1952. Its purpose was the breakdown and eradication of race-specific jobs.

Association for Merit Employment, Box 1, Folder 4, Indiana Historical Society, Indianapolis, Indiana.

13. AME records for 1963 do not include how many applicants sought employment.

14. Association for Merit Employment Collection, Indiana Historical Society, Indianapolis, Indiana.

15. Guichard and Brown, *Blacks in the City.*

16. Sam Jones, executive director of Indianapolis Urban League, interview by the author, tape recording, Indianapolis, Indiana, March 30, 1993.

17. Relying on census data to track employment statistics is both rewarding and frustrating. No other source adequately enumerated the percentages and types of jobs held by African Americans. However, the census categories lump workers into broad categories, and for some occupations, such as day laborer, there are no reliable records.

18. United States Bureau of the Census, *Fourteenth Census: Population;* Spear, *Black Chicago;* Trotter, *Black Milwaukee.*

19. United States Bureau of the Census, *Fourteenth Census: Population.*

20. Ibid.; Kenneth L. Kusmer, *A Ghetto Takes Shape: Black Cleveland, 1870–1930* (Urbana: University of Illinois Press, 1976), 75n.

21. The census only examined individuals who were employed or actively seeking a job, hence the disparity between the high level of employment and the relatively low number of women actually in the workforce.

22. U.S. Census Report, Indiana, 1940; U.S. Census Report, Indiana, 1950; U.S. Census Report, Indiana, 1960.

23. Robert G. Barrows, "A Demographic Analysis of Indianapolis, 1870–1920" (Ph.D. dissertation, Indiana University, 1977), 248–251.

24. Trotter, *Black Milwaukee,* 46.

25. United States Bureau of the Census, *Fourteenth Census: Population.*

26. Ibid.

27. Barrows, "A Demographic Analysis of Indianapolis," 169.

28. *Indianapolis Times,* September 26, 1949.

29. Emma Lou Thornbrough, *Since Emancipation: A Short History of Indiana Negroes, 1863–1963* (n.p.: Indiana Division, American Negro Emancipation Centennial Authority, 1964), 80.

30. *Indianapolis Recorder,* January 21, 1950.

31. *Indianapolis News,* November 11, 1949.

32. Thornbrough, *Since Emancipation,* 81; Williams, interview; Andrew J. Brown, interview by the author, tape recording, Indianapolis, Ind., March 10, 1992.

33. Thornbrough, *Since Emancipation,* 77–78.

34. Ibid., 79.

35. *Indianapolis Times,* September 26, 1949.

36. Clarence Wood, interview, Indiana University Center for the Study of History and Memory, Bloomington, Indiana.

37. Lawrence and Mary Brookins, interview, Indiana University Center for the Study of History and Memory, Bloomington, Indiana.

38. *Indianapolis News,* November 12, 1949.

39. *Indianapolis News,* November 12, 1949.

40. Richard L. Rowan and Lester Rubin, with the assistance of Robert J. Brudno and John B. Morse, Jr., *Opening the Skilled Construction Trades to Blacks: A Study of the Washington and Indianapolis Plans for Minority Employment* (Philadelphia: University of Pennsylvania Press, 1972), 125.

41. *Indianapolis Times,* September 27, 1949.

42. *Indianapolis Times,* September 26, 1949.

43. *Indianapolis Recorder,* April 8, 1950; *Indianapolis Recorder,* May 6, 1950.

44. *Indianapolis Recorder,* September 23, 1950.

45. *Indianapolis Recorder,* September 9, 1950.

46. *Indianapolis Recorder,* December 13, 1958, February 25, 1950, March 25, 1950.

47. *Indianapolis Recorder,* March 18, 1950.

48. Frederick Doyle Kershner, Jr., "A Social and Cultural History of Indianapolis, 1860–1914" (Ph.D. dissertation, University of Wisconsin, 1950), 169.

49. Ibid., 193–195.

50. *Indianapolis Times,* March 26, 1961.

51. Walter Reuther Collection, Box 264, Folder 3, Wayne State University Archives of Labor and Urban Affairs and University Archives, Detroit, Michigan.

52. Thornbrough, *Since Emancipation,* 77.

53. Ibid., 80.

54. Lawrence and Mary Brookins, interview, Indiana University Center for the Study of History and Memory, Bloomington, Indiana; Alberta Murphy, interview, Indiana University Center for the Study of History and Memory, Bloomington, Indiana.

55. Lawrence and Mary Brookins, interview.

56. Ibid.

57. The black unemployment rate for 1960 was 8.5 percent while the white unemployment rate was 4.9 percent. Indianapolis Chamber of Commerce, "The Economically Disadvantaged and their Employment in Indianapolis," Indiana State Library, Indianapolis, Indiana.

58. Lawrence and Mary Brookins, interview, December 5, 1995.

59. Stephen Arnold Wandner, "Racial Patterns of Employment in Indianapolis: The Implications for Fair Employment Practices Policy" (Ph.D. dissertation, Indiana University, 1972), 176.

60. James H. Madison, *The Indiana Way: A State History* (Bloomington: Indiana University Press, 1990), 240–245; Matthew Welsh, *View from the State House: Recollections and Reflections, 1961–1965* (Indianapolis: Indiana Historical Society, 1981), 94–95, 191–196; Indiana, Acts of 1961, Chapter 208, Section 208.

61. Wandner, "Racial Patterns of Employment in Indianapolis," 118–119.

62. Ibid., 123.

63. Ibid., 122–124.

64. Ibid., 124.

65. Harold Hatcher left Indiana to take a position in the Office of Economic Opportunity in South Carolina.

66. Wandner, "Racial Patterns of Employment in Indianapolis," 151.

5. Building a Fence around the City

1. William Blomquist and Roger B. Parks, "Unigov: Local Government in Indianapolis and Marion County, Indiana," in L. J. Sharpe, ed., *The Government of World Cities: The Future of the Metro Model* (Chichester, England: John Wiley & Sons, 1995), 77.

2. C. James Owen and York Willbern, *Governing Metropolitan Indianapolis: The Politics of Unigov* (Berkeley: University of California Press, 1985), 43.

3. The Democratic Party benefited significantly from the large and vibrant African American voting community. The African American population was a bulwark of Democratic Party strength. Warren E. Stickle, "Black Political Participation in Indianapolis: 1966–1972," *Indiana Academy of the Social Sciences, Proceedings*, 3rd series, IX (1974): 113–120.

4. *Indianapolis Recorder*, November 7, 1959; *Indianapolis News*, December 27, 1968; *Indianapolis Star*, January 6, 1969; Owen and Willbern, *Governing Metropolitan Indianapolis*, 44.

5. *Indianapolis Times*, July 14, 1963.

6. Carl R. Dortch, "Consolidated City-Government Indianapolis-Marion County, Indiana Style," Indiana Clipping File, Indiana State Library, October 1974, 3.

7. Ibid., 47–48.

8. Tobe Johnson, *Metropolitan Government: A Black Analytical Perspective* (Washington, D.C.: The Joint Center for Political Studies, 1972), 3.

9. David M. Lawrence and H. Rutherford Turnbull, III, "Unigov: City-County Consolidation in Indianapolis," *Popular Government*, November 1969, 18–20; Rodney L. Kendig and Charlene Caile, "Consolidated City-County Governments in the U.S.," *American County*, February 1972, 8–23.

10. Owen and Willbern, *Governing Metropolitan Indianapolis*, xvii.

11. *Indianapolis Star*, January 5, 1969.

12. Richard G. Lugar, "The Need for County Leadership in County Modernization," speech delivered to the 34th Annual Conference of the National Association of Counties, Portland, Oregon, July 28, 1969. Found in Indiana Academy of the Social Sciences, *Proceedings*, Third Series, Vol. IV, 1969.

13. "Interparty arrangements guaranteed at least one Negro seat on the council." Lawrence and Turnbull, "Unigov: City-County Consolidation in Indianapolis," 19.

14. Ibid., 46–48. In Indianapolis government circles, groups like RAC were fairly common. One of the most outstanding of all the characteristics of Indianapolis's urbanism was its persistent substitution of organized cooperation for individualism. Kershner's assessment was drawn from an analysis of the Gilded Age era in Indianapolis, but this tradition of non-elected coalitions affecting policy would continue well into the next century. Kershner, 423.

15. Owen and Willbern, *Governing Metropolitan Indianapolis*, 49.

16. Dortch, "Consolidated City-County Government Indianapolis-Marion County, Indiana Style," 2.

17. Owen and Willbern, *Governing Metropolitan Indianapolis*, 49–51.

18. Marcus Stewart, Jr. of the *Indianapolis Recorder* was a member of the Task Force. Garnering the *Recorder*'s support was indispensable. The newspaper was widely read in the black community. Although Stewart offered cautious support, one of the *Recorder* columnists, Andrew Ramsey, criticized the creation of Unigov.

19. Owen and Willbern, *Governing Metropolitan Indianapolis*, 61.

20. Ibid., 92.

21. The assertion that Unigov was possible because proponents did not need to achieve a referendum does not mitigate other causal factors, namely, the political alignment that placed Republicans in crucial political posts, and the skill Unigov's supporters exhibited. Yet it was the need for a referendum that forestalled many other consolidation efforts. James F. Horan and G. Thomas Taylor, Jr., *Experiments in Metropolitan Government* (New York: Praeger Publishers, 1977), 62.

22. "Uni-Gov—Workable but . . . ," n.d., Metropolitan Government Clipping File, 1970–

79, Indiana State Library, Indianapolis, Indiana; Kendig and Caile, "Consolidated City-County Governments in the U.S.," 18.

23. Metropolitan Government Clipping File, 1970–79, Indiana State Library, Indianapolis, Indiana.

24. Lawrence and Turnbull, "Unigov," 20.

25. *Christian Science Monitor,* March 31, 1969.

26. Owen and Willbern, *Governing Metropolitan Indianapolis,* 93–95.

27. *Indianapolis Recorder,* January 18, 1969.

28. *Indianapolis Recorder,* February 22, 1969.

29. Quoted in Owen and Willbern, *Governing Metropolitan Indianapolis,* 95.

30. *Indianapolis Recorder,* January 4, 1969.

31. *Indianapolis Recorder,* February 29, 1969; Johnson, *Metropolitan Government: A Black Analytical Perspective,* 1–2.

32. *Indianapolis Recorder,* February 8, 1969.

33. Ibid.

34. Stickle, "Black Political Participation in Indianapolis," 114–115.

35. Owen and Willbern, *Governing Metropolitan Indianapolis,* 186–188.

36. Ibid., 88–99.

37. *Indianapolis Recorder,* October 9, 1971.

38. *Indianapolis Recorder,* November 23, 1971.

39. The *Recorder* editors specifically rejected John Neff. They urged readers to vote for all of the Democratic candidates except Neff. *Indianapolis Recorder,* October 30, 1971.

40. Owen and Willbern, *Governing Metropolitan Indianapolis,* 180–186.

41. Blomquist and Parks, "Unigov," 79, 81.

42. Robert Voss Kirch, "Metropolitics of the 1971 Unigov Election: Party and Race," Indiana Academy of the Social Sciences, *Proceedings,* 3rd series, VIII (1973): 139–140.

43. Stickle, "Black Political Participation in Indianapolis," 113–114.

44. Henry J. Richardson to Gene Sease, president of Greater Indianapolis Progress Committee, July 31, 1973, Box 14, Folder 17, Henry J. Richardson Collection, Indiana Historical Society, Indianapolis, Indiana.

45. Kirch, "Metropolitics of the 1971 Unigov Election," 139.

46. *Indianapolis Recorder,* April 6, 1971.

Conclusion

1. David Stoelk, director, "Indy in the 50's" (produced by WFYI Television, Indianapolis, Indiana, 1995).

2. Oscar Robertson, *The Big O: My Life, My Times, My Game* (Emmaus, Pa.: Rodale, Inc.), 50.

3. Stoelk, "Indy in the 50's."

4. Robertson, *The Big O,* 52.

5. Ibid., 54.

INDEX

RICHARD B. PIERCE is the Carl E. Koch II Assistant
Professor of History and Associate Director of African and
African American Studies at the University of Notre Dame.